# Your Best Year Yet!

# Your Best

# Year Yet!

A Proven Method
for Making the Next Twelve Months
the Most Successful Ever

JINNY S. DITZLER

WARNER BOOKS

A Time Warner Company

Warner Books, Inc., 1271 Avenue of the Americas, New York, NY 10020
Visit our Web site at http://warnerbooks.com

Printed in the United States of America

ISBN 0-446-52532-4

To Tim,
with my love and deep appreciation.

But there is such a thing as genuine love,
which is always considerate. Its distinguishing
characteristic is, in fact, regard for personal dignity. Its
effect is to stimulate self-respect in the other person.
Its concern is to help the loved one become their true self.
In a mysterious way such love finds its truest realization
in its power to stimulate the other to attain their
highest self-realization.

ROMANO GUARDINI

# CONTENTS

# ACKNOWLEDGMENTS

One of the biggest blessings of writing this book is the opportunity to say "Thank you" to the people who have taught me and helped me so much. Without them, this book and the work I do would have been impossible.

To all the participants in all the Best Year Yet workshops—you have proven it works and inspired me to pass it on.

To each of my clients: You have trusted me and allowed me to share so fully in your life—in your presence I have learned the secrets I share here.

To my friends Jock and Susie, who said "Do it!" loud enough for me to hear.

To our support group, who have been my British family for the past eighteen years.

To my greatest teachers: Werner Erhard, who gave me the keys to my power; John-Roger, who opened my heart; and Lew Epstein, who showed me how to let myself be loved.

To my courageous colleagues and partners in Results Unlimited and The Results Partnership, who carved the path for transformation in the U.K. in the tough years before there was a demand for it.

To Celia Brayfield, who wrote about her coaching sessions with me long before it was safe to do so.

To Val Corbett, creator and producer of *Executive Coach,* who saw something in me I hadn't seen myself and then helped me to share it so powerfully.

To my partners in Best Year Yet, Limited, and Your Best Year Yet, LLC, who share the dream of getting this process to as many people as possible as quickly as possible.

To my British agent, Bruce Hyman, whose persistence and insights have raised the level of this pursuit far beyond anything I could have done myself.

To my American agent, Denise Marcil, whose courageous intelligence and know-how took me places I *never* could have gone on my own.

To my editor, Jessica Papin, and her team, who have helped make my vision for this book a reality.

To my parents, Leo Eugene Anderson and Katherine Thomas Anderson, whose keen intelligence and strong will I have inherited but whose love has meant everything.

To my wonderful big family who have encouraged me at every step, been proud of me, and helped me believe in myself.

To my son Charley, who long ago swallowed the lessons in this book and has made me so proud.

To my son Jeff, a great friend who keeps me laughing and has been an immense help in so many, many ways.

And, most of all, to my husband, Tim, who has loved me through everything and given me the joy of sleeping with my biggest fan!

# WELCOME

I invite you to have your best year yet—year after year—for the rest of your life.

The Best Year Yet experience is designed to reach the core of how you think and perform, and to empower you to new levels of personal effectiveness and fulfillment. In a three-hour process of self-discovery, you stand back, take stock, and then plan the next year of your life. The exercise of answering ten simple questions helps you to clarify your thinking and make sure your next year is the best it can be. At the end of your personal workshop you'll have a simple one-page plan to guide you through your next twelve months.

This format has been used by thousands of people over the past twenty years, and together we have shaped and simplified the annual life review and planning process to a point of profound power. Yes, we've been able to improve our ability to make things happen and many, many of us are more successful financially, in our careers, and in our relationships. But more important, we've taken the time to gain an overview that offers us a better chance of giving meaning to our lives and what we do. It brings us to a new level of consciousness and awareness in the way we live and direct our own lives.

Many, many people have carried out this exercise on an annual basis for years; it has helped them to create a fundamental shift in their lives and the satisfaction of achieving the results that really matter to them. As one friend said so eloquently, "I saw that I wasn't living the way I want to be and now I've stopped postponing a lot of things that are dear to me."

So many have learned to take the lead in their own lives—it's a beautiful sight. I've used this same process for myself and I'm astounded at what I've achieved and how I've grown as a person. Every year since the first has somehow, in some way, been my best year yet. So, as I often say to participants in the workshop, "If a schoolteacher from Nebraska can do it, so can you!"

Again, I welcome you and invite you to join us on your own journey of increasing self-respect that comes from living your life in a way that reflects what matters most to you.

## How to Use This Book

Both the public and corporate workshops are half-day events, but over the years many people have been doing the workshop on their own, usually taking about three hours to get through the ten questions. Watching them succeed so well on their own helped me realize that this really can be a simple do-it-yourself process.

Many people create their Best Year Yet plan in January so they can plan the calendar year ahead. But the process of reflection and planning can been done at any time of the year with equal success. Don't think of this as a book that's only about January through December—if you're reading it now, then now's the time to answer the questions, believe you can do it, and get on with it.

This book is divided into three parts:

| Part One | An introduction to the principles on which Best Year Yet is based, as well as sharing the experiences of many people who have participated in the process over the years. |
|---|---|
| Part Two | Each of the ten questions has its own chapter in which I review the background material and provide further explanation to help you answer each question for yourself. |
| Part Three | Your own Best Year Yet workbook with space for you to answer each of the questions and write your own one-page plan for the next twelve months. |

You have your own style of doing things, and depending on what that is, pick your approach to your best year yet from these options:

1. Turn immediately to Part Three and start answering the ten Best Year Yet questions. If you want help or explanations as you go along, turn to the chapter in Part Two that relates to the question you're working on.

2. Read Part One and Part Two as preparation for your workshop, perhaps making notes as you read. When you've finished, set aside three hours and write your answers to the questions in Part Three.

Whatever your choice, enjoy the journey!

# The Turning Point

The idea started on New Year's Day in 1980, when my boyfriend (now my husband), Tim, and I woke up in our flat in London. We'd been working in the U.K. for less than a year and living together only a couple of months, having met shortly after we both arrived from the States the previous spring.

Perhaps I needed a bit of distraction, as I'd given up smoking the night before and had made such a public fuss there was no turning back. Or maybe it was the thought of the new decade ahead. Who knows? But for the first time in ages I began to think a bit more seriously about the year ahead. And before we even left our bed, I suggested that we run a marathon that year, and Tim agreed.

This was the only goal I remember setting that year, probably because we hadn't decided to stay together and thinking ahead was a tentative business—we weren't really at the point of planning a life together.

We picked the Paris Marathon, scheduled for May. The goal may not seem unusual today, but 1980 was a year before the birth of the London Marathon, and the sight of a runner on the road in England—particularly a woman—was reason for staring and pointing.

We started to train and, although we'd been in the habit of jogging a couple of miles several days a week, we were told we needed a new regime that would work us up to over fifty miles a week in the last month before the marathon. Gradually we began to lengthen our prework circuit of Bishops Park in Fulham to runs over Putney Bridge, up the towpath, under the Hammersmith Bridge and on, until we reached whatever point was halfway to our target time for the day, then turned back toward home along the same route we'd come. It was hard work.

By mid-March we began to see the end of the winter mornings and were starting to feel better about it all. As we talked with friends, some of them became interested, and soon what began as a ridiculous conversation on the first day in January took on a life of its own. In the end nearly a hundred of us went to Paris in two buses, had a great time, and raised thousands of dollars for charity.

But it was painful beyond belief—I thought it would never end, and for Tim it was even worse. We ran the entire marathon side by side. At Mile 20 he was in such agony and so delirious that after a water stop he started running back toward the starting line! But we did it. And the feeling of confidence and elation at having set and achieved such an outrageous goal lasted long past the finish line. I learned, above all, how to keep going, and in doing so found new strength and ability I didn't even know I had. I would never have discovered this if I hadn't forced myself to go for this goal.

By the following New Year's Day in 1981 Tim and I were engaged to be married, still in the same rented flat, and starting to think about planning the year ahead. We'd had a good year. The marathon had definitely been a big thrill, but little else had really changed. Late in 1980 we'd decided to try to buy a place of our own and in the process discovered that between us we had a *negative* net worth. It hadn't proven easy for either of us to build a career in London, and although we weren't too depressed about it all, the path ahead was not clear.

When the time had come for me to transfer back to the United States, I had left a good job because I wanted to stay with Tim, but hadn't found another one. We'd also had many long conversations about whether he really wanted to stay in the business world. We were happy together and having a good time, but we were broke most of the time, allowing ourselves one monthly treat of dinner out at a local restaurant. But looking back it's easy to see that New Year's Day in 1981 was really a turning point for us.

It's on this day that the Best Year Yet workshop was really born, although I didn't start to lead the workshop for others until the following year. As we sat down to plan the coming year, common sense guided us to create this process. Before we started to think of the year ahead, it seemed natural to review 1980 and what had happened for each of us. Expecting the worst, we both found that we'd accomplished far more than we thought. We started to feel a bit more enthusiastic about ourselves and what lay ahead—an experience which, by the way, has proved to be the case for nearly everyone who has participated in the Best Year Yet program over the years.

By the end of the day we each set over a hundred goals. Nineteen eighty-one was definitely the best year yet for both of us—we were married, ran three more marathons, and each of us started a business, both of which are still going today.

Still, we ended the year with a low "score" because the sheer number of goals we had set made the achievement of all of them impossible. When it came time to pass the idea on to others, it was obvious that having so many goals made it impossible to keep track of even half of them! The exercise has now been simplified to help us find our top ten goals, and the whole process takes about three hours.

But setting our goal of running a marathon that first morning of 1980 was the start of a new way of living for us. And once I turned the process into a workshop, more people had the chance to do the same for themselves; together we all found out a great deal about how to use our brains and our common sense to learn from the past year and make the best of the year ahead.

Tim and I have used the annual exercise in good times and in bad, taking time out every year to make sure we do it, no matter what. Just going through the process of coming up with our top ten goals for the next year creates a powerful focus, even though there were some years when I would go for months before looking at the goals again. No two years are the same, obviously. Some years the focus of the goals is on money, some years fitness and well-being, some years relationships with family, some years working with a favorite charity, and some years just facing up to challenges I couldn't possibly have predicted the year before.

We certainly haven't achieved all the goals we've set, and we've hardly tracked our progress with robotic precision the way we always felt we should. But Best Year Yet has continued to provide a framework for our lives, building year on year, making sure we at least have the chance to learn the lessons of our past year and move on to our next goals.

Sometimes when we come to the review at the end of the year, we feel like the Torville and Dean of personal planning; other years it takes quite a bit of courage to look back. But we've kept at it for all these years now and it's made all the difference. There's no similarity between my life today and my life then, in terms of either the goodies available to me or the quality of my life. I'm blessed with a lifestyle that's beyond anything I imagined as a child.

It's the discipline of working the Best Year Yet questions year after year that keeps us going and helps us continue to grow and learn. Things have not always been as good as they could have been, but at those times I've learned to do my best to apply myself in the ways I've described in this book. Over the years, with the help of so many, Best Year Yet has evolved into a simple ten-question process that can be used by anyone, anytime. While I hope I've learned by now that I have no right to impose my beliefs on others, I'm enthusiastic about passing this program along because of what it's meant for me and so many who have participated in it.

The best part for me has been my growing sense of myself, the confidence I now have, my appreciation for my particular talents, the way I'm able to work through life's knotty problems, and the deep feeling that I'm doing a bit better all the time at living a life that's consistent with what I believe. These are the most important things that have come from the exercise of annual evaluation and planning.

Turning around to face life's most painful challenges has given me a growing personal strength and a deeper sense of who I am. And every time I'm able to do that myself, my ability to coach and encourage others to do the same is increased. *If I can do it, you can do it.* The effectiveness of my work with people keeps increasing as I get better and better at practicing what I preach. But I'm still learning and always will be. I once heard a radio interview with Luciano Pavarotti in which he said he's never stopped taking singing lessons and doesn't intend to stop learning until the day he dies.

Inspired by Best Year Yet, Tim and I have done a little personal version nearly every week. We both work long hours and often don't see each other much during the week; several years ago this was eroding deeply into the quality of our marriage. The way we confronted that challenge, eventually not only restoring our love but deepening it, is one of the best examples of the transformation we've achieved.

Several years ago we starting having what we call our Friday night party, just the two of us. We get a bottle of wine, put on some music, and sit and talk with each other until we catch up.

To balance the effect of some painful times, we started taking turns making toasts to the best things that had happened over the past week. Even in the worst weeks, there are those little miracles and things to be grateful for. It makes such a difference to remember to focus on how lucky we are rather than on what a struggle it all is.

And this is the real gift. If somehow we lost everything, we'd be strong enough to withstand it and start again or let it all go and live in a tent. I honestly believe that the inner strength we've developed can't be taken away and that we'll be all right no matter what happens.

Above all, my motivation in writing this book is to make this kind of true success possible for you—to help you design a more meaningful life for yourself by giving you the means to become the master of your own destiny.

I've seen so many people who have made changes in their lives by taking the time to think about what they really want and then taking steps to make it happen. Watching them over the years has inspired me to write about Best Year Yet and make it available to more people. You're never too old nor too young to make the coming year your best yet.

# Your Best Year Yet!

# PART ONE

# Three Hours
# to Change Your Life

# The Principles Behind Best Year Yet

## Goal Setting

Successful businesses set goals and plan ahead. They know that in order to generate the kind of important changes and growth they're looking for, they must identify their priorities each year and then focus the energies of their people in such a way that these goals are achieved. The secret of realizing this kind of success for ourselves is the same—setting goals and planning our lives a year at a time. In this way we too can deal with the bigger issues, address the concerns that really matter to us, and make the kinds of important changes we really want to make.

You know about goals—we all do. We've set them and even been successful in achieving many of them. By the age of eight or ten we begin to get an idea of what we want in life. A picture begins to form in our minds of a degree, a job, a car, a house, a family . . . and as we move through our teenage years our goals become even more clear to us. Soon we're twenty-five or thirty or thirty-five and we've achieved many of these early goals and trust we're on the way to the others. And new goals are already forming in our minds.

However, as life goes on, goal setting becomes a more casual and far less specific process—wants and desires seem to occur and plant themselves in our minds almost before we realize it. We don't often set goals within a one-year time frame, and we rarely make a conscious choice about which of our goals is most important to us. We find ourselves in pursuit of goals before we've really taken the time to think them through, determine their real cost, or consider what's really important to us.

Maybe you're in the habit of coming home exhausted and turning on the television rather than sitting at the table and sharing a meal with a loved one or listening to your favorite music or reading that book you've been longing to get to—or planning the next year of your life.

After the initial spurt of growing up and becoming an adult, most of us don't stop to think about goals in the same serious way we did when we carefully planned our education, our career, or our first home away from our parents. We begin to follow our noses, reacting to circumstances and meeting our immediate needs and those of the people around us. All this becomes a full-time job and more. Time goes by, and soon we begin to feel that our lives are out of control and there's nothing we can do about it. Things that matter most to us aren't getting enough attention, and life gets frustrating. We feel we're no longer in charge of our own lives.

In one of my recent "bibles," Sogyal Rinpoche says,

*If we look into our lives, we will see clearly how many unimportant tasks, so called "responsibilities," accumulate to fill them up. One master compares them*

*to "housekeeping in a dream." We tell ourselves we want*
*to spend time on the important things of life, but there never*
*is any time.*

There are things that have to be done, and we feel we have no choice about it. And by the time we are finished doing everything that has to be done, we're too tired to think of doing anything else. Gradually we become cynical about things like New Year's resolutions and lifetime goals. Why bother?

We feel that our most frustrating situations and problems are out of our control—there's nothing we can do to change things, so we give up and try our best to cope. The thought that we could actually *do* something about our deepest frustrations just doesn't occur to us anymore. We give up on creating a life that is more meaningful and fulfilling and settle for what we have. We give up on ourselves and our ability to make things happen.

Yet part of us is unwilling to settle—the part that wakes up in the middle of the night worrying and contemplating the things that matter most to us: *What am I doing here? What have I really accomplished? Why can't I make better use of my time? What can I do to take better care of my family? When is it going to be my turn? Surely there must be more to life than all these worries and frustrations? What's the point?*

Or perhaps when you're listening to music or watching a play or film, you're lifted out of your busy life and moved to remember who you really are and what you want for yourself and those you love. And then morning comes or the play ends and these important questions fade into the background, covered over by ritual doubts and fears. The day takes over, as it always does, and you don't take the time to think about what you really want or how you could make it happen if you did.

**The strongest motivation for doing Best Year Yet is that you find the way to live your life so it shows what really matters to you—so you are true to yourself.**

Probably you, like many, get frustrated and say, "I've had enough!" You set a goal and start to do something about making it happen, but then your drive fizzles once again. Too often our most important goals are not set with the belief that they can really be achieved, so that before long we lose momentum. We've forgotten how to keep our attention on what we've accomplished rather than on our failures and mistakes. We forget how to live our lives remembering what we do well and therefore stop building confidence in ourselves and our ability to succeed.

We human beings have an enormous capacity to remember our failures while forgetting our successes. Memories of our failures cause us to lower our sights and lessen our opinion of ourselves. We become frozen in the shadow of our biggest problems and can't turn around to face them. While in parts of our lives we may be strong and capable, we seem to lose potency in the face of the concerns that cause us the most pain.

Here are examples of the kinds of problems I'm talking about—many of them have been shared by clients, and many I've faced myself:

- "My relationship with my teenage son has gone astray, and that brilliant, sparkling little man who used to run and jump on my lap and tell me everything seems lost to me. If I let myself think about it too long, I would weep."

- "The success I've struggled toward for so long is here, but I'm working harder than ever and there's no time to enjoy it. The days go by so quickly and I'm not making the best use of the time I have. The dream for which I sacrificed so much has dissolved."

- "The body that used to bound up stairs and give me the energy to work and think for hours and hours seems to have run out of steam, but there's no time to get it back into shape—and it's probably too late anyway."

- "I seem to spend most of my time at the office in meetings, handling last-minute emergencies or dealing with other people's problems. I can never seem to get around to sitting back from my job and thinking about the future and how we're going to get ourselves out of some of these messes once and for all."

- "I want to make my mark, I want my life to matter. How can I find more fulfillment in my job? Should I leave this job and find another one that gives me a better chance to do this? Why don't I devote at least some of my time to causes I care about?"

- "I feel as if I'm chasing my tail most of the time. There's always a deadline to meet and it's always tomorrow. I know I should plan ahead and stop procrastinating as much as I do, but I don't have time!"

- "What's wrong with me? Why isn't there one person in the world to love me and share my life? I don't want to be alone."

- "I feel stuck in this job—I'm going nowhere fast. They don't realize how good I am and probably never will. But I really don't know how to find something with a better future. I can't figure out what to do, so I do nothing."

- "Why can't I find some time to 'stop the music' at least once a day to meditate and contemplate and let the noise of the 'to do' list be silent for a moment? How do I stop the mental chattering when I do?"

- "What's driving my life—me or my debts? Most of my vital spirit and energy is spent in the pursuit of money and I don't know how to get off this merry-go-round of survival."

- "The person I married years ago who loved me so deeply is now too busy and preoccupied to really look at me or listen to me. But now I'm so frustrated, angry, and resentful that I don't really care whether he does or not."

The longer we go on putting up with these painful situations and not reclaiming our dreams, the more we diminish in our own eyes and then lose our ability to make the changes that mean the most to us. At some point we stop thinking about the possibility of changing any of it: *That's just the way it is; I mustn't grumble.* The idea of even setting a goal such as *Start enjoying the success I've achieved* or *Put some romance back in my life* or *Find a new job that gives me a chance to prove myself* simply never occurs to us anymore.

Sometimes we make promises to ourselves, such as:

- Tonight I'm going to go home and not touch the television.

- This weekend I'll take my son out for a drive and see if I can't begin to get closer to him.

- Next Monday the diet starts!

- Tonight I'm going to the gym on the way home.

- First thing tomorrow I'm going to look in the classifieds and pick a few jobs I could go for.

- On the way home today I'm going to stop and get some flowers and a bottle of wine . . .

But too often we don't keep these promises, and every time this happens we become somehow weaker and believe in ourselves a little bit less. It is this way of thinking about ourselves that stops us more than our failure to think ahead or set goals. We come to believe that we're not capable of making the changes that matter, and therefore we stop setting goals and planning ahead in any meaningful way. And the life we really want for ourselves drifts out of reach.

**Our limiting beliefs about ourselves become like brick walls in front of us, keeping us from even thinking about how to make the big changes or set the big goals.**

Once we've come to this point in life, we begin to protect ourselves with familiar defenses and excuses, such as:

- Once something's gone bad, you can't really change it.

- Why think about it; I know I can't afford to have what I want anyway.

- Goal setting and thinking about what I want is such a selfish and self-absorbed business.

- I want to keep my options open!

- Once I get through this busy time, I'm really going to take time to sort myself out.

- It's boring to know where I'm going and what's going to happen next.

- I'm not willing to sacrifice now for something in the future.

- I can't stand the thought of trying and failing one more time.

- You can't teach an old dog new tricks.

- I really can't be bothered.

And so, while we wouldn't think of getting in a car and not knowing whether we're going to Newark or Nashville, we gradually become passengers in our own lives. Years go by and we never get out of the car to see how it's doing or where it's going. We simply sit in the backseat preoccupied by our busy, busy lives, which are moving too fast to allow time to stop the car, take stock, consider alternate routes, or set goals to change direction—in short, to get back into the driver's seat.

## Best Year Yet

The Best Year Yet three-hour process forces us to get out of the car and take a better look at ourselves and our lives. What have we accomplished on this trip? What do we do well? What have we learned about traveling? Have we taken any wrong turns? And most importantly, how far have we come?

This exercise, although not always easy, becomes more of a

pleasant and uplifting experience than a painful process of recrimination. It helps us face these important questions and take stock. The biggest challenge is finding three hours in a life where there is no time to do this kind of thing. But if we want to be more responsible about creating our lives rather than merely coping with our lot, we must do Best Year Yet *instead of* something else.

This is the most difficult part for most of us. Just don't *do* that thing you *think* you have to do right now. Do Best Year Yet instead. We've often held our public Best Year Yet workshops on a Saturday, and it's easy for the people there to realize that in order to come to the course they had to forgo the weekly laundry, the Saturday errands, cleaning the house, writing the letters, paying the bills, seeing their friends—or whatever else they usually feel they *have* to do on a Saturday.

Even though they will have spent a big part of the day at the workshop, they can see that they'll get the clothes washed and somehow get food in the house. Those things always get done. It's not *those* things that are the problem; finding time to plan your life is the problem. But once it's done, it makes far more difference than getting the laundry done. So grab yourself by the collar, get a pen and paper, and make yourself sit down and answer the ten questions. Or take a lesson from the people who have come to the workshop: Book three hours with a family member, colleague, or friend, and do the exercise together.

The process asks you to look back over your past year and then begin to think about the coming year by asking yourself these ten Best Year Yet questions:

1. What did I accomplish?

2. What were my biggest disappointments?

3. What did I learn?

4. How do I limit myself, and how can I stop?

5. What are my personal values?

6. What roles do I play in my life?

7. Which role is my major focus for the next year?

8. What are my goals for each role?

9. What are my top ten goals for the next year?

10. How can I make sure I achieve them?

Best Year Yet is like successful gardening. While I'm not the first person to suggest a strong correlation between life and gardening, think about it for a minute: *We must prepare our soil before we're ready to plant the seeds we want to grow in the next year.* As we answer the first two questions, we look to see what grew and what didn't grow last season. The third question helps us discover what we've learned and what we want to remember for next year.

Reviewing successes and failures in the garden involves little guilt or self-recrimination—a good lesson. We take a moment to enjoy the successes of the past year so we can be strengthened by them rather than weighed down by our failures. In other words, let go of your disappointments and failures—pull them out as you would weed your garden. Why should they crowd the space and negatively influence what happens next year?

The fourth question is the last step before planting. Here we fertilize the soil—enriching every clump by working in the lessons and the intentions we have for the year ahead. Enriching the earth in your garden means making sure that the way you're thinking about yourself will contribute to your success rather than poison your soil. Imagine what would grow in a garden polluted with a strong sense of failure. The secret of Best Year Yet is planting seeds in rich soil.

**Too often people set goals without preparing the personal environment for those goals to succeed. Best Year Yet, refined by so many over twenty years, clearly and efficiently prepares this environment.**

So the process starts with thinking back over the past year of your life, remembering what you *did* accomplish, and focusing on the causes for celebration. Yes, you. This first step allows you to balance your views of the past year and of yourself. It's so easy to remember our failures: promises not kept, times we let others down, New Year's resolutions that didn't last a week, weight not lost, miles not run, mornings we didn't meditate, letters not written, closets not cleaned, books not read, friends not seen, lost hours with our children . . . here our memories are so vivid.

Being human, we forget what we've done well and how much we have accomplished. We lose sight of the strengths and gifts we do have and then fail to use these gifts to make the changes we want to make. We don't take steps toward the goals that are most important to us because we don't think we can. *But for all of us, the problem is not a lack of ability. It is a matter of focusing the ability we have while at the same time renewing our belief in ourselves.*

Reviewing your past successes gives you the chance to balance the way you think about yourself and, having learned from both successes and failures, let them go. In doing this, as you begin thinking seriously about the year ahead, you are reminded that you *do* have the ability to set and achieve new goals. While it may be uncomfortable to think about yourself in this way, to do so is to know yourself again and begin to feel, as you did at age eight or ten, that you can be the master of your own destiny.

**More than anything, Best Year Yet is about starting to believe in yourself again and becoming much tougher in the face of life's biggest challenges. The approach helps you to use your common sense and intelligence in new ways to create a happier life for yourself.**

I remember Jane Fonda's story of how hard it was for her (she was then in her mid-forties) to get past her terror and learn to do a back flip into a lake for her role in *On Golden Pond*. Her costar Katharine Hepburn watched her, and when after many days filled with hours and hours of practicing she succeeded, said to her, "Everyone should know that feeling of overcoming fear and mastering something. People who aren't taught that become soggy."

# "Don't Let Weeds Grow Around Your Dreams"

This quote from H. Jackson Brown's *Life's Little Instruction Book* is one of my favorites and reminds me of people I know who have followed Miss Hepburn's advice. I'd like to tell you about a few of the friends and clients who have had the courage, heart, and discipline to use the lessons of Best Year Yet in their lives.

It may sound a bit glib and easy when their lives are reduced to such short "success stories," but do your best to move past that point of view and become aware of how each in their own way decided to make a change in something that was important to them. Also notice if you find it much harder to believe these experiences than the earlier examples of people's problems.

One woman had left her husband for a confirmed bachelor. However, six months later this new love stopped telling her how much he cared for her; after five weeks passed without him saying that he loved her, she was afraid she'd made a big mistake. When she realized her focus was not on the result she wanted but rather her fear, she set a goal: "Develop a great relationship with Sam and learn to remember how much I am loved."

She was able to keep this focus and dissolve her fears; within a year they were married.

---

A highly successfully entrepreneur in his late fifties wanted to move on to something new and more exciting but felt guilty leaving the loyal people in the company he'd built up over the previous twenty years—and was worried that at his age he couldn't really afford to go out on his own. His goal: "Finish with my company and be ready to launch my new venture by the beginning of the year."

He found and developed a new person whom he trusted with his company and his people. Now that he's moved on and started his new business, he's filled with new enthusiasm and energy for what he's doing.

---

One woman, having spent her life taking care of her five children and supporting her husband's career, longed to find a way to express herself and be more creative in her life, but had long ago lost the confidence to figure out how to do it. Her goal: "Find a way to build a successful business that allows me to express my sense of style and creativity."

It took her a while to identify what type of business she wanted and then how to get started. But finally she opened a store selling the kind of jewelry and clothing she wore and loved.

---

A talented journalist was earning a small weekly wage as a television critic for a national daily newspaper and struggling with a ten-month-old daughter, a huge mortgage, and growing anxiety. She found that she never liked doing things she was afraid of and was afraid of pursuing what she wanted most. Her goal: "Build a career doing what I love to do that pays me what I'm really worth."

She approached the project of her personal transformation with great determination and intelligence. It didn't happen overnight, but she worked steadily and consciously and today is a best-selling author currently working on her sixth book.

---

A couple had worked together for years to grow a successful business, which now kept them overly busy and exhausted doing work neither one of them enjoyed. When early in the recession the bank put on intense pressure, they felt the burden of the business more than ever. Out of a strong sense of duty and a good deal of fear, they were both continuing to invest a lot of money and time in the growth of the business when that was the last thing they wanted for themselves. Their goal: "Move on to a work life that is more satisfying, creative, and rewarding for both of us—and make this move as soon as possible."

Once they allowed themselves to set the goal they really wanted, the business began to turn around and they found a friendly buyer so they could back out and set off on their own again.

---

A successful company president had begun to feel like an old man before the age of fifty because of severe back and leg pain that kept him from doing much that he loved. He was deeply depressed because he felt like a prisoner in his own body; he was used to being able to pursue a wide range of business and personal interests without such restrictions. His goal: "Feel physically, mentally, and emotionally free to live my life as I choose."

He pursued this goal with relentless discipline, attacking it from many angles—medical, emotional, mental—and within months was walking straighter and moving without pain.

---

One couple had suffered severe money problems for years—both actors, it had become harder and harder for them to get work. They had been forced to sell their home and move to a smaller one; soon they feared they would have to take their children out of the private school that meant so much to them. At the beginning of one year, they made a strong commitment to "Put money problems behind us once and for all."

Their approach was relentless, calling on friends for support and talking with experts to help them get things sorted out. Within a couple of months one of them was offered a major role in an international television series.

----

A young woman had left nursing for a sales job in order to make more money and better use of her skills, but had just finished a year when she hadn't achieved her sales target. She was concerned she might lose her job now that the recession had really hit her company. Her goal: "Make this my breakthrough year."

Even though it was the toughest year the company had ever known, she started shifting her perception of herself and doing things she'd previously not tried. By the end of the year she had cracked her target and became Salesperson of the Year. She was promoted to Client Services Director for the business and began using the same people skills that had made her a good nurse to manage people in a business setting.

----

A designer was doing well in her career but was miserable in a relationship where she was comfortable but that she felt she had probably outgrown. She desperately wanted to get married and have children, but with this man? She was afraid that if she let this one go, she might not find the one she really wanted. Her goal: "Move on and find the man I'm going to marry."

She found the courage to end her relationship and move out on her own. Although uncertain, she kept her eye on the goal and eventually met a bright young lawyer with whom she could develop a much stronger bond; they married and now have two beautiful daughters.

Within each of these successful people is an ordinary person who found the courage to act—to face the big challenges and make their dreams come true. They built the inner strength to stop worrying about their problems and direct their focus toward the goal they wanted to achieve. They took the time to step back from the busyness of life and all its issues to put their attention on the goal that, when achieved, would make the most difference to them. And they did their best to avoid the pitfalls of explanation, complaint, and excuse so they could keep going until they got what they wanted.

# My Best Year Yet

As we've said many times so far, it's a challenge to set serious goals about things that really matter. If you're reading this book then you know I've finally been successful in achieving my goal of writing a book, a dream I've had for as long as I can remember. But nothing happened about this goal for years and years and years. In fact, even though I've been doing Best Year Yet for myself since 1980, it didn't make it to my list of top ten goals until recently. It just seemed an impossible dream to me, so I didn't give it any serious thought. Much longing, believe me, but no serious thought.

And even though I was leading Best Year Yet workshops and coaching others to have their big dreams come true, this goal lay dormant and untouched beneath a pile of regret and resentment. There was always a reason why now wasn't the time:

- I'm too tired at the end of the day and on the weekends.

- My business partners and clients need me to be doing something more important and far more urgent.

- The onset of menopause has stopped my brain from functioning.

- My writing a book wouldn't contribute to the direction in which we want the business to go.

- It would be a waste of time doing something that probably wouldn't earn us any money.

. . . and on and on.

The thread you can see running through my reasons for not writing is the mind-set *I'm a victim of circumstances beyond my control.* This is a common theme for me, and certainly one I've often spotted in other people. Over the years the tune in my head has been the same, though the key has changed from time to time: *I'd love to write. I'm probably a great writer. I really have something to say but I can't because* _____ (fill in the blank from the list above).

Several years ago I even subscribed to a magazine for writers with the hope that it would stimulate me to do something, but every month when another issue arrived in the mail I was filled with guilt and frustration. I piled them in a neat chronological stack by my bed so that when the time came I could read them, learn about writing, and motivate myself to get started. But that time never came.

Until one New Year's Day, when Tim and I spent the day with our friends Jock and Susie.

At some point in the day we were talking about Best Year Yet, and I was scribbling down the ten questions for them to use, explaining how the process worked and telling them about the good time we'd had doing the exercise a couple of days before with our son Jeff, who was with us during his Christmas break from college. (He'd started the exercise with little enthusiasm as he listed four accomplishments and twenty-six disappointments for his past year! But later he told us how good it felt having let go of some of the terrible memories he had of the past semester: *That's done. I need to move on.*)

Then one of them said, "You know, you really should write a book about this!" We laughed at the tired suggestion; we all know each other well and sometimes tease one another about dreams gone moldy. Mine is the well-known book. But somehow they got through to me that day, and I began to get excited about writing in a way that was different for me. I felt that they really did want me to write the book, and they convinced me that Best Year Yet was an important idea that could help a lot of people. This was music to my ears. And so I started to believe in myself more seriously and redid my goals for the year, changing number four on my list of top ten goals to: *Write my first book and find a fabulous agent and publisher.* And when I next spoke to Jeff, he looked at me with his smirk and said, "Yeah, Mom, just do it!"

When I got past my initial euphoria and actually tried to start writing, I was stopped for more than a month by another stack of limiting beliefs:

- I'm probably not nearly as good as I think I am.

- Every book I want to write has already been written.

- I can't stand the thought of people reading what I've written—they'll probably laugh at me behind my back and never tell me.

- This is all so trite and stupid.

- How can anyone be expected to write a book when they're already working fifty to sixty hours a week?

- No publisher will want to publish anything I've written anyway.

All this with a husband who kept encouraging me to write a book, telling me that he knew it would be a best-seller.

 **We love our limitations! We must, because we certainly don't want to let them go.**

# Victim of Circumstance?

We become comfortable thinking of ourselves as smaller than our problems, feeling a victim of circumstances, and blaming others for the fact that we don't have what we want. It's not that other people aren't terrible sometimes, but becoming their victim makes us powerless. Hopefully it's easy for you to see that my blaming other people and situations for not being able to write my book robbed me of this goal for years. I had made myself impotent. And yet it's just a small example of something we can see around us everywhere.

There is always someone and something to blame in our lives. Blaming becomes a habit, and not an easy one for any of us to give up. It's a comfortable old friend. Just yesterday I asked my friend Mary what she was doing in the coming three-day weekend. She said, "I'm going to the country to visit my aunt and her family. The prediction is for the weather to be beautiful, but with my luck it'll probably rain." What luck? Who says? How crazy to wallow in the perverse satisfaction of such statements whose empty reward is being able to say, "See, I knew it!" or "I told you so." We can hear evidence of this attitude everywhere if we listen for it, but we're so used to it we're largely unaware of it or its cost. Catching ourselves in this self-defeating approach to life, as I had to do with my writing, is the only way out.

Too rarely do we hear anyone say,

- "This weekend is going to be great!"

- "Leave it to me, I'll deal with it."

- "I'm sorry, it's my fault. It won't happen again."

- "We've made a couple of mistakes but we'll keep going until we get it right."

But the alternative to playing the victim is to become tougher inside ourselves and start taking personal responsibility for our own lives. I understand how hard it can be. But Best Year Yet works, and it goes on working, year after year, dream after dream. This is especially clear to me as I sit here tapping away on my computer, enjoying the process of passing it on.

As far as I can tell, life is more about learning than anything, and again and again I learn the lesson of the Chinese proverb that says, "If we don't change our direction, we are likely to end up where we are going."

# Ready or Not?

By now you've read quite a bit about me and people I've known. Now it's time to take a moment to think about yourself. The more aware you can be of yourself as you begin this process, the more successful you'll be. Answer the following questions as honestly as you can. No one's watching.

## Life So Far

Circle either T or F, depending on whether the statement is true or false for you:

T   F   There have been times in my life when I have set and achieved goals.

T   F   When I take the time to think about it, I'm proud of what I've accomplished so far.

T   F   While I feel I have much to be grateful for, something is missing and I'd like to find out what it is.

T   F   I know I have more potential than I've used so far.

T   F   I can remember times in the past when I kept going regardless of setbacks and made something happen.

T   F   I know that I've lost confidence in myself over the years, but I'm not quite ready to give up.

T　F　I know that if I tackled at least one or two of the issues that trouble me most, I'd be much happier.

T　F　I find it easier to remember my failures than my successes, and I see how this has caused me to stop believing in myself as strongly as I once did.

T　F　It troubles me that although I have strong personal beliefs and values, the way I've lived my life so far hasn't reflected these as much as I'd like.

You don't have to be a rocket scientist to figure out that the more T's you have circled, the better chance you have to succeed in setting plans and making them happen. How many did you circle?

## Personal Beliefs and Values

Check those statements that express your personal beliefs and values:

☐　I am responsible for myself and what happens to me.

☐　Although I sometimes resist the idea, I'm aware that even a bit more discipline could make a big difference in my life.

☐　I believe that anything is possible if you set your mind to it.

☐　"As ye sow, so shall ye reap"—or, What goes around comes around.

☐　Keeping a positive attitude is vital to my success.

☐　It's wise to ask for help when I need it.

☐　It's all right to make mistakes because it shows I'm trying.

- [ ] The more successful I am, the more important it is to give back in some way.

- [ ] I'm committed to the happiness of my loved ones.

- [ ] It's very important to me to live up to my personal beliefs and values.

Obviously in this section the information is personal and there are no right or wrong answers. However, I believe most of these statements would be accepted by people who have become truly successful. What matters most is to know what *you* believe in and what *you* value.

Our sense that something is missing comes at those times when we're off the course set by our beliefs and values. One of the ten Best Year Yet questions explores this area more fully.

 **What motivates most of us far more than material success or recognition is our desire to be true to ourselves and live our lives in ways that demonstrate our personal values and beliefs.**

## Excuses I Have Known and Loved

Check the ones you've used in the past.
I really want to do things differently, but I can't because . . .

- [ ] I want to keep my options open.

- [ ] Once something's gone bad, you can't really change it.

- [ ] Goal setting and thinking about what I want is such a selfish and self-absorbed business.

- [ ] I passed my "sell by" date a long time ago.

- [ ] Once I get through this busy time, I'm really going to take time to sort myself out.

- [ ] It's boring to know where I'm going and what's going to happen next.

- [ ] If I fix my mind on a goal, I'll miss other exciting opportunities when they present themselves.

- [ ] You can't teach an old dog new tricks.

- [ ] I can't be bothered.

To be honest, I'd be suspicious of anyone who didn't check most of these excuses. Welcome to the human race. The challenge for all of us is to become more aware of the times we're using these excuses rather than doing what we want to do to move ourselves forward. Be especially wary of any you see as statements of truth rather than excuses. They have the power to stop you.

## How Motivated Am I?

On a scale of 1 to 10, with 10 being the highest, rate yourself on the following:

\_\_\_\_\_ I am committed to making positive changes in my life.

\_\_\_\_\_ Planning a year ahead and setting goals for myself makes sense to me. I'm ready to give it a try.

_____ I can count on myself to do what I need to do this time.

_____ I know a great deal about what I need to do to change my life.

_____ It matters to me that I live up to my personal beliefs and values.

_____ I'm willing to do whatever it takes to make this process work for me.

_____ There are other people in my life who would benefit if I took the time to plan the next year of my life.

_____ Even though I'm afraid to confront some of my problems, I'm ready to do it.

_____ I'm now ready to use my abilities and my intelligence more fully and courageously.

_____ I'm going to set aside three hours in the next week to answer the ten Best Year Yet questions. No matter what.

_____ TOTAL SCORE

Total your score on motivation and refer to the chart below to see how ready you are for your best year yet.

90–100   Congratulations. It's possible that life will never again be the same for you.

70–89   Although you may need to push yourself from time to time, you could be on your way to your best year yet.

51–69   It's hard to tell what's going to happen. You're not quite sure whether you're really ready to get into the driver's seat.

If your score is below 50, you've just told yourself that you're not ready to make the most of the information in this book. Either improve your approach or wait until you're feeling more confident. However, any of you who scored a 10 on the last statement have the best chance of all.

# Just Do It

In over twenty-five years of working with people, I've seen one big difference between those who truly succeed in making things happen and the ones who don't: Those who do, act.

They think of an idea and they move on it. They get a feeling that something could work and they take the steps to try it out. They take a course and they find the discipline to put what they've learned into practice. They read a book, find an idea they like, and they take steps to use it in their lives. They hear about a meditation that could decrease their stress level and give them a stronger sense of who they really are and they set aside the time and get started. They just do it.

So if you're one of these people, stop now and turn to Part Three, where you'll find the Best Year Yet workbook. Make a cup of coffee or pour a glass of wine, turn on some music, and start writing your answers. It's that simple. And three hours from now you'll know even more about where you're going and feel more motivated to get there. Just make yourself do it—the way you usually do.

According to Stephen Covey, the first habit of highly effective people is to *be proactive*. In other words, rather than letting life happen to you, make it happen. Even if you don't recognize yourself as one of those people who just does it, you could *become* one of them simply by moving straight to the questions and getting started on *your* best year yet.

Some people are born to "just do it"—they seem to have come packaged with a strong inner drive or compulsion to succeed, and they move full steam ahead. But most of us have had to learn a great deal in order to do a better job designing our own lives; we were made rather than born. I'm certainly one of these. Compared to the consciousness with which I now live my life, I spent most of my early days in a sleepy fog, feeling jerked around by life but "doing my best given the circumstances."

So, even if you're not one of the high-drive people described above, you're not out of the race. You've already achieved so much in your life, and I hope you appreciate that about yourself. But in order to make the best use of this book you need the discipline to sit down and write your answers to the ten questions.

 **The truth is, you already know a great deal—**

**more than you think you know—about what to**

**do to change your life for the better.**

The trick is doing it, taking that first step, making it happen. And yet often we don't. While it's important to find out what stops you and why (which we'll explore in later chapters), what works best is just getting on with it. Understanding your limitations can come later.

Answering the ten deceptively simple but powerful Best Year Yet questions can make all the difference. It's not always an easy exercise, but in the process of answering the questions you'll learn a lot about yourself, how you make things happen, and how you hold yourself back. You'll begin to see how to build a more meaningful life for yourself, and soon you'll be looking forward to the year ahead. I promise. Just do it.

**One more word about getting on with it: If you're wondering, "Is this book the one that will really help me?", the answer is, it certainly could be. It's up to you. As you well know, it's not enough to buy the book. In order to stop floating from one resolution to another or drifting from one good intention to the next, you need to act.**

Most of us trap ourselves by not being willing to take the necessary steps to be the masters of our own lives, yet we'll be damned if we'll let anyone or anything serve as our master for us in the meantime! The result? No one's in charge. We get nowhere. Every bit of true progress I've made in my life has come from really listening to a loved one, a teacher, or an author, and having the discipline to practice his or her lessons until I have learned them. Action and follow-through are everything.

There's another prevalent mind-set that can stop us from making the best use of the modern repackaging of ancient wisdom so popular in the past twenty to thirty years: cynicism. Those with this attitude attempt to take the intellectual high ground over any discipline of self-improvement or personal transformation by labeling it "silly ineffectual nonsense" or "psychobabble" and displaying a general snobbery toward anyone who tries to support us in making positive change in our lives. This approach is just another path of avoidance that stops us doing what we want to do. I know; I thought this way for years.

So, if you've decided that this book could help you and you're ready to get going right away, turn to the questions and get started. Or if you are someone who prefers a more deliberate approach, that works too, sometimes better. This book is not about the quick fix or creating overnight miracles, although for some of you it might do that. Whoever you are, if you feel there are changes you'd like to make and you scored well on motivation, now is the time. Just do it!

PART TWO

# The Ten Best Year
# Yet Questions

# What Did I Accomplish?

*Increasing your self-esteem is easy. Simply do good things
and remember that you did them.*

JOHN-ROGER

## The Good News

No one's looking. Start to tell yourself what you feel good about.
Maybe no one noticed some of your finest moments, but *you* did.
Make a note. Maybe others did notice. Those count, too.

- Did you get through another year of school? What were the
  best times?

- Did you move into a new home? Did you decorate or repair
  the one you have? Did you clear out a lot of old stuff? Did
  you take things to Goodwill?

- Did you start a new job or get a promotion? Have you been
  doing a better job at work? What deserves a pat on the back?

- How much money did you earn in the last year? Did you pay
  off some of your debts? Did you manage to put some more in
  the savings account or invest it?

- Did you get married? Have a child? Did one or more of your children have a good year? Did you help him or her over a troubling time? Have you been a better parent this year?

- Did you finally start to get fit? Are you exercising even a little more? How do your clothes feel compared to the beginning of the year—a little looser? Have you started to eat more healthily?

- Have you been in touch with old friends more this year? Did you make some new ones? Have you been a better friend to the ones you have?

- Did you start to do more enjoyable things? Attending concerts? Reading? Theater? Films? Seeing friends?

- Are you doing a better job of keeping in touch with family members and friends?

Even if some of these questions don't spark memories of your best moments, force yourself to think about your achievements and times when you were proud of yourself, did something well, or put a problem behind you. Make a note. Bragging is allowed.

**When you find achievements to celebrate, you nourish your spirit and motivate yourself.**

I'm not asking you to invent something but merely to notice what you *did* achieve and then write a list of the good news for the past year. Think about the headlines, but get beyond that—everything counts, big and little. Look at the sample list at the end of this chapter, which illustrates how important it is to remember as much as you can about what you've achieved.

Use this experience to get closer to a new part of yourself—the strong inner part that really keeps you going day after day. It may be uncomfortable; most of us are much more at home with our failures. It's so much easier to talk with friends about things that aren't going well, to have a good whine. But the stretch into new territory is worth it.

There's nothing phony about this; what we're talking about goes beyond mere positive thinking. Positive thinking is too often the same as papering over the cracks and pretending things are different than they are. That's not what we're doing. As you answer these questions, be absolutely honest with yourself. No one else need ever see what you've written, so you're safe. Whatever happened last year, tell the truth. Just don't get stuck thinking it was far worse than it was, remembering the struggles while forgetting the triumphs.

Balance your perception of yourself. I'm asking you to realize that the truth is far better news than you've been letting yourself believe. You're laying the groundwork for your best year yet; if you start by thinking about the good news, you'll be in far better shape to make it happen. I'm asking you to be responsible for how good you are and to put the whip away!

Yes, it would be wonderful if others noticed how good you are and how well you're doing. But that's not yet the world we're living in. So, as a first step, do it for yourself, and then you'll be much more willing and able to do it for others.

## Why Start with Accomplishments?

The first question of Best Year Yet leads you in a positive direction and gives you the chance to rebalance your perception of yourself and what you've achieved in the past year. Almost without exception, people's initial thoughts about the past are negative. An invisible magnet draws us to the bad news and the failures. Unless we stop to think about what really happened, we assume that there is far greater cause for disappointment than celebration.

Rarely do we stop and think about we've achieved in a day, let alone a year. Imagine that you've started a day by making a "to do" list of everything you need to do. Say the list is ten items long and at the end of the day you've achieved eight out of ten. Do you say "Well done," or even "Not bad"? Good for you if you do—but most of us just feel guilty that we didn't achieve *the other two*. Our consciousness is snared by the bad news, the things we didn't get done. Again our self-esteem diminishes, and we're probably not looking forward to the next day as a result.

This is no accident. We live in a world inhabited by people doing the same, and it's catching. Well-meaning friends and relatives can have a negative view of things, and it becomes embarrassing to be positive or optimistic. We're told that bad news sells newspapers and attracts more television viewers. We live in a negative culture that focuses on the bad news, so it's easy to make an unconscious assumption that there's *more* of it. But that's not the case.

**Awareness brings its own reward. Shifting your attention to what you have accomplished in the past year awakens your "Can Do!" attitude and gets you back in touch with your ability to make things happen.**

Most people find when they answer this question that they're pleasantly surprised to remember how much they have achieved over the past year. Rather than a few meager achievements in a field of failures, it's often the opposite. We start here so that you can see this for yourself and be energized and uplifted by this perspective of yourself.

This exercise will help you see the past in a new light and start to rebalance the effects of your environment—that of your own making as well as the wider one in which you live. Your own accomplishments are the best and most authentic reminder that you *can* create your own future and become more the master of your own destiny.

So Best Year Yet starts with a pat on the back.

## How Did We Get This Way?

But where did it all begin? How did we learn to be so much more critical than positive?

I believe we were taught from the time we were small. Not by a carefully conceived curriculum designed to teach us to whip ourselves mentally and emotionally—to flog ourselves for what we haven't done, for mistakes we make, for our failure to achieve a higher standard of performance and behavior. No one set out to create a population so hard on themselves that they feel incapable of making important changes in their lives. Nevertheless the impact of parents, teachers, and bosses has been as effective as if they had planned it all.

Of course the reality is that many of us *are* parents, teachers, or bosses—and some (like me) have been all three. Most of us are victims and perpetrators at the same time. So I make these points with a great deal of humility and compassion for each of us and for whatever drives us to interact with others in any way that leaves them feeling smaller or less able. Few of us want this outcome as a result of our interactions with our children, our friends, our students, or our employees.

Yet in spite of the best of intentions, the messages we give and receive are far more negative than positive. Most parents spend far more time telling children what *not* to do than what *to* do; they have developed a habit (probably through being the children of their own parents) of correcting far more than praising. We are carefully taught the sin of pride and of feeling good about something we've achieved.

While I'm not recommending that we walk down the street with our chest puffed out letting everyone know "I'm the greatest!", we need to do something to stop operating with this unbalanced view of ourselves that robs us of our spirit and our belief in ourselves. The effect of this phenomenon reaches every part of our lives. So while feeling better about ourselves is a private matter, it's also a vital one. But it's not easy.

Even as I sit here writing this book, making all these wise points, I often catch myself being scolded by the negative little voice inside my head: "This is interesting stuff but you're *way* behind. You should be getting a lot more written today," or "Why go back and rewrite that paragraph? You're just avoiding moving on to the parts you haven't written," or "This is okay—at least you'll have an interesting Christmas present to give your family next year even though no one else will read it." I've learned by now that this little voice is so strongly programmed that I may hear it until the day I die. But my job is to flick it away and keep encouraging myself with more accurate and empowering messages, such as "You're doing fine. This is going to be great, just keep going." At the end of the day, I don't know how many people will read this book, but if I'd listened to this negative little voice I'd have stopped writing and would never know.

The cost of this negative conditioning is enormous. What

motivates you more: a correction or a compliment? Which boss do you want to work for: one who constantly points out the error of your ways, or one who spends time noticing what you're doing right? If you're like me, the answer is apparent. Running in the first London Marathon, I'll never forget the difference in my reaction to the messages we received from supporters along the way. "Keep going, don't stop now!" made me angry, while "Great job! You're brilliant!" made me feel like a star.

Obviously we want to be told when we need to improve or have failed to perform to the required standard. Bosses wouldn't be doing their jobs if they failed to do so. But we need far more than this if we're going to do our best and feel like bringing *all* of ourselves to the office in the morning as well as to the business of directing our own lives.

I like visual models to explain concepts and give an easy reminder of important lessons. The Cycle of Productivity on pages 42 and 43 demonstrates the flow of four phases of activity, from the time we first think of doing something to the moment we've finished it.

The first of the four segments is the beginning, when we come up with the idea and then decide to do it and get started.

The second section of the cycle involves the greatest amount of time—this is the period when we're actually doing all that needs to be done to carry out the idea step by step.

The third section is challenging for many. This is the phase where we do the last thing to finish the project or bring the idea to fruition. We tie up all the loose ends so we can say, "That's it, I did it! Nothing more to do."

Usually we get stuck in one of the first three segments. There are those who seem to stop at the starting gate. We have lots and lots of ideas but rarely get them off the ground. Or we have far more ideas than we could ever carry out but don't take the time to

# CYCLE OF PRODUCTIVITY (COMPLETE)

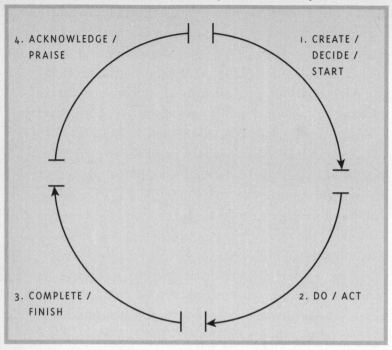

4. ACKNOWLEDGE / PRAISE

1. CREATE / DECIDE / START

3. COMPLETE / FINISH

2. DO / ACT

decide which ones are not worth the effort and toss them out. So they sit on a list or nag us in our minds, making us feel guilty.

Some of us get stuck in the second phase—doing, doing, doing—neither fully completing a project nor taking ourselves back to the drawing board to create new possibilities. You can recognize this in yourself by the piles of paper, mail, magazines, books, crafts in progress, and so on, that surround you.

If you're one who slows down in the third segment, you find it difficult to finish anything. As a result there are many incomplete projects in your life. You may have made a good start on a book, a sweater, cleaning out your car or desk drawers, decorating . . . but what have you *finished* lately?

# CYCLE OF PRODUCTIVITY (INCOMPLETE)

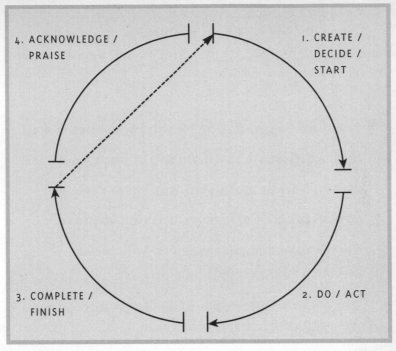

4. ACKNOWLEDGE /
PRAISE

1. CREATE /
DECIDE /
START

3. COMPLETE /
FINISH

2. DO / ACT

Obviously, wherever we get stuck, it slows us down, getting in our way both mentally and emotionally.

But by far the most important lesson of the Cycle of Productivity comes in segment four. Too many of us simply go straight from the end of the third segment back to the starting line without taking a pause for acknowledgment, pats on the back, thinking about what happened, or learning from it. Our eye is always on what's next or what isn't yet completed, and before long we feel as if we're running on fumes—below the empty mark! We forget to stop for gas. We don't feel like we're getting anywhere and we experience little satisfaction.

This model reminds us to take time to appreciate what we've

accomplished and how far we've come. By doing this, when we get back to the starting line, whether it's a big new challenge or just tomorrow's "to do" list, we feel more energized and positive and work more productively than ever. We feel far more energetic, and our momentum picks up again.

> ◈ **Praise and appreciation for the good news make all the difference to us. We feel stronger and more naturally motivated, and there's less of that needy part of us always trying to prove ourselves and hoping someone will notice.**

That's why the first question in the Best Year Yet process asks you to remember your accomplishments.

## Others' Experiences

Here is an example of a woman who looks as if she's had a difficult year, yet as you can see is able to put some of her memories in the context of accomplishments.

> **WHAT DID I ACCOMPLISH?**
>
> 1. Cooked at least two hundred dinners for my family.
> 2. Didn't gain any more weight—at least.

3. Got a good promotion at work.

4. Read ten novels and five high-quality nonfiction books.

5. Decorated Sarah's bedroom.

6. Stayed within the household budget and saved over $1,000.

7. Learned to type.

8. Took care of things at home and work while I've been exhausted.

9. Been much more positive and supportive with the kids.

10. Didn't throw a tantrum when our vacation was canceled.

11. Entertained our friends a bit more.

12. Paid off my credit card every month.

Several of my clients have been able to look back on some of the toughest years and remind themselves how well they did considering how horrible the circumstances were. They still named each year their best year yet because of the amount of personal growth they achieved while changing gears and learning new skills to deal with new circumstances.

After a difficult year it's even more important to acknowledge and appreciate yourself. Focus your outlook on the bright side. We can define our lives in any way we choose, regardless of what happens. The challenge is to live life in the context of gratitude instead of complaint.

QUESTION TWO

# What Were My Biggest Disappointments?

*Mistakes are the portals of discovery.*

JAMES JOYCE

## The Bad News

So, what were your disappointments in the past year? Pick up your pen and write them all down. Remember the times you disappointed yourself and didn't do what you had hoped to do. Recall the instances when others didn't do what you wanted them to do.

- What dreams didn't come true?

- What expectations weren't fulfilled?

- Did you want a raise? A promotion? A new job?

- Did you promise to get yourself out of debt, only to get in deeper?

- Were you hoping to bring a new love interest into your life?

- Did you want to get married to the person you're with, but it didn't happen?

- Were you hoping for the birth of a child?

- Did you lose a loved one either to separation or death?

- Do your clothes fit the same or even a bit tighter? Did you start an exercise program and let it lapse, and do you now find yourself disgusted with the way you feel?

- Did someone who was kind and loving to you simply stop?

- Were you hoping for a great vacation, only to see the plans change?

- Were you hoping to go back to school?

- Did you want more time to yourself? To read? To meditate? To paint? To write? To think? To stare into space?

- What else?

There's more value than you can imagine in just writing these disappointments down. While it seems something to avoid—who wants to think about all this?—I've always felt a great weight lift from me when I gave myself time to think about what happened rather than pretending it didn't hurt so much.

**Telling the truth to yourself provides a great release, and doing it inside the Best Year Yet context shows you the way ahead.**

Some of us are more comfortable with our failures than with our successes, so we keep them around. Cozy old friends. We sometimes feel that the answer to the second question in Best Year Yet is the *real story* while the successes are a bit contrived. Again, that's not the case. For others, it's probably necessary to move out of the comfort zone and tell the truth about your disappointments and failures in this way. In any case the rewards for doing so are great.

Don't forget that our view of ourselves has become unbalanced. While in answering the first question about accomplishments you had to go through the discomfort of congratulating yourself, you now have to accept the fact that your failures are not really an accurate reflection of who you are and what you're capable of. (You'll have the chance to explore more of this dynamic in depth when you answer the fourth question, "How do I limit myself, and how can I stop?")

And watch out for another pitfall: *I've listed five accomplishments, but there are eighteen disappointments on my list. See! I am a failure!* It doesn't matter in the least. Don't add meaning and significance to what's happened in the past. That's just a good way to attract more of the same so you can be right about how inadequate you are. Avoid the lifetime pursuit of arguing for your limitations. Learn to stop invalidating your accomplishments and focusing on your failures.

Think about it. Who do you know who achieves everything on their list? Who do you know who achieves every goal they set? Do you *know* anyone who *knows* anyone who does? Have you read about or heard about anyone who lived without failure or disappointment? No, but you think *you* should or you're trailing in the human race.

◈ **What happens, happens. The only thing we _can_ control is how we respond to what happens to us. The successes are great and we can enjoy them. And the failures are, well, great character-builders.**

# Pull the Weeds

You can't grow the way you want if you don't pull the weeds of your disappointments and failures. Certainly you can't avoid them, but once they've grown you must clear them away in order to make room for something new. Answering this question helps you do this.

Looking at your disappointments and letting them go can move you to a place where your self-assessment is no longer based primarily on failure—you can start to heal yourself mentally and emotionally, as you heal yourself physically when you are ill.

But to answer this question you must tell the truth. I don't mean that you have to walk around telling people about how badly you've done, but tell the truth to yourself—that's the important thing. You may have been hiding your failures from yourself for some time. If so, this is a good chance to stop doing that. What we hide from runs us.

For the purpose of your Best Year Yet exercise, you don't have to tell others about your shortcomings, although at some point you may want to talk with someone in order to pull the weeds in your relationship with them. But for me I find that it's enough just to write everything down, absolutely everything, so that I can get it out of my system. I've never shown my entire list of disappointments to anyone in the twenty years I've been doing this, but it's made all the difference just to get them down on paper.

# Excess Baggage

Letting yourself get weighed down with a sense of failure and hopelessness keeps excess baggage in your life. You don't need it, and it's harmful because it makes life difficult and robs you of your ability to move as quickly as you'd like—just as if you were carrying around a couple of heavy suitcases.

And the joke's on all of us. No one else can see your excess baggage, yet there's an unconscious assumption that all your limitations are obvious. But others don't see your mental movie of the past and the spin you've put on it. They simply don't know your version of history, and those who do are probably far more charitable and respectful of you than you are of yourself.

Remember the times when you've heard friends or colleagues bemoaning their failures or talking about how difficult it is to have what they want? Sometimes it's hard to be sympathetic because you can't understand why they don't just *do* it. You see them as capable and talented people and it's difficult to see what's stopping them.

But what's stopping them, more effectively than a brick wall would, is their excess baggage. They're dragging it into the present and letting it dissolve their sense of what's possible in the future.

We make our excess baggage even heavier by adding negative

emotion—anger, resentment, regret, sadness, and so on. Of course, these are understandable and human responses, but when they cause you to feel less able than you are—or worse, a victim of circumstances—you get stuck. The downward spiral begins and can degenerate into the kind of bitterness that erodes your character and leads to keeping a mental crime log on others, your circumstances, and your environment. Woe is me, yes. But what good does it do you?

**What happened, happened. The best you can do for yourself is to examine what happened and then do everything you can to neutralize your experience. Get rid of the extra weight that comes from the negative emotion. Save yourself. Stop carrying all that weight around. Lighten your load and lighten up.**

You can get rid of the negative filter through which you view the world and yourself. You've been walking around wearing a pair of glasses in need of a good cleaning. Letting yourself answer this question fully helps to clear your vision and enables you to see things as they are. I'll talk more at length about this concept in discussing Question Four, "How do I limit myself, and how can I stop?", but the first step is to take a look at the past year of your life and examine the disappointments you've experienced.

THE
PAST

THE
FUTURE

## The Past

In my grandma's house there was a wooden sliding door between
the living room and the dining room. When we pulled the brass
handles, the two halves of the door came together, separating the
two rooms. Imagine yourself standing in front of that closed door-
way. The panel on your left is your past and the panel on your right
is your future. Most often this is the way we view our lives.

In this picture there's not much space for the present moment—a thin line, but no view—because our minds are so full of
the past and the future. The secret of happiness is to open a crack
between the past and the future and live life in the moment we're
in. Every time I've been able to achieve this, I've had a sense of

freedom and flow. But how do you do it? How can you get your guilt about the past and your anxiety about the future out of your mind long enough to have a renewed sense of yourself in *this* moment in time? As one of my teachers often said, "Stop trying to drive with your hands on the rear-view mirror!"

> **When you find yourself dwelling on the past in a way that makes you think less of yourself or your ability to make change, let go of the thought and focus on what's happening <u>right now</u>.**

You really have only three possibilities when it comes to dealing positively with negative aspects of your past:

1. Forgive.
2. Forget.
3. Learn.

Forgiving yourself is often the hardest. Yet you've done your best. Forgive yourself and have compassion for yourself. In order to forgive others, you need to have compassion for them as well. Can you understand and appreciate what it's like for them? Why did they do what they did? Did they get out of bed in the morning with the intention of hurting you or making life difficult for you? Probably not.

Some failures and disappointments we can just forget. As I

look at my list each year, there is often an item that reminds me of quite a long tale. So difficult and so painful, but so what? It's over and now it's just a story. Merely making the list and looking at it automatically releases much of the negative emotion associated with some of the things on it. And while we may not be able to forget our failures, at least we can ease their sting by neutralizing the effect of the negative emotions we've attached to them.

The best way to deal with the past is to learn from it, and that's the purpose of answering the third question, "What did I learn?" The principal value of our mistakes and our failures is to learn from them. As William Saroyan said, "Good people are good because they've come to wisdom through failure."

# Let Go

Again, the purpose of the first two questions in Best Year Yet is to rebalance our sense of ourselves and make room for new possibilities. Releasing our hold on the whip of resentment and regret is the first step. Most often these are the two underlying components of our disappointments and the dynamic that keeps them in place.

One of the ways to trigger your mind about the disappointments of the last year is to ask yourself, "What or whom do I resent?" Although you may find that the answers come flooding into your mind, it's sometimes difficult at first to let ourselves write them down.

It's hard to admit to some of those feelings that at face value may look so petty and small. And it's difficult to let ourselves take a deep breath and face the pain they represent. But the opportunity of moving on from the pain and heartache caused by these feelings is worth all the discomfort of taking the time to look them in the eye.

The anger, the sadness, the feelings of powerlessness and hopelessness drain us of our vital life energy. Once we start to neutralize these feelings, we're empowered to do something positive about the source of the problem.

 **We have the ability to move on to a happier state—letting go of resentment and its cost to us has been proven again and again to be a foolproof path to greater success, health, and general well-being.**

What good is the resentment doing you? Is holding on to the resentment making things better? What has been the result so far of holding on to that resentment? It's really so funny when I catch myself with a death grip on my resentment: I'm not going to let go until . . .

- they apologize.
- they realize the error of their ways.
- they finally listen to me.
- they do things my way.
- they stop driving me crazy!
- etc., ad nauseam.

And in the meantime, I'm *not* going to let them off the hook. But who's miserable and who's stuck in the past? There's no possibility of growing anything different in a garden filled with this kind of poison.

So make some notes in response to the question about resentment, and as you write your answers, think to yourself, "Let go!" Imagine pulling each weed as you go.

And then there are the regrets—things you wish you hadn't done and things you wish you had. Well, it's too late to do them *last* year, but it's not too late for next year. You've got another chance. When thinking about last year, ask yourself, "What do I regret?" Add your answers to your list for Question Two. Later you can come back to some of these and consider turning them into goals for next year.

But for now let them go. Remember their only real value now is in their lessons. And in hindsight many of these experiences, both resentments and regrets, no matter how painful and difficult, were just what we needed at the time in order to grow and learn and move on.

## Others' Experiences

One of the advantages of doing this process with others or in a workshop is that you have the stimulation of their experience. In conversation, they let you know a bit about how they're answering these questions. To give you a chance to see how others have answered this question, here are two examples of some others' partial answers.

The first is written by a young man. Notice how his list is quite a mixture. Facts and feelings are combined and were written down as they occurred to him. Remember, whether something on your list is clearly one of your failures or a disappointment that wasn't your fault but affected you deeply, write it down.

## WHAT WERE MY BIGGEST DISAPPOINTMENTS?

1. Gained fifteen pounds.

2. My father died.

3. Ending my relationship with Sue—still not over it.

4. Earning the same as a year ago in spite of the fact that I deserved to get a raise.

5. Haven't done anything to find another job that I'd like better.

6. Trip to Europe never materialized.

7. Joined a gym and only went seven times!

8. Didn't spend more time taking care of Mom—weeks go by and I forget to phone her.

9. Sex life is nonexistent.

10. I never get a break—my health is beginning to suffer.

11. Feeling really ugly and stressed out.

12. Let my credit card debt build up to over $3,000.

The second example is that of a woman. Her list reveals that she's more neutral about some of the items on the list than others.

It comes out in the way she's expressed herself—a perfect reflection of her mixture of disappointments for the past year of her life. The important thing is that she's taken the time to get it all down on paper.

## WHAT WERE MY BIGGEST DISAPPOINTMENTS?

1. Didn't meditate past the first month.

2. Feeling tired and drained—don't want to cook another dinner.

3. Bitter about how busy Peter is—always late, working on the weekends. How will he ever get to know his children?

4. Want to get back to work, but have failed to do anything about it—I'm losing my nerve.

5. No time to myself.

6. Having the romantic weekend with Peter in San Francisco canceled at the last minute.

# What Did I Learn?

*Men stumble over the truth from time to time but most pick themselves up as if nothing had happened.*

SIR WINSTON CHURCHILL

## Lessons Learned

Look back over your answers to the first two Best Year Yet questions to see what you've learned. In reviewing Question One, what you accomplished, what possible lessons do you see?

**What you've achieved so far is the greatest source of information for you. The same strengths, skills, and qualities you used to achieve them are still available for next year.**

Take a minute to answer the following questions:

• What was the secret of my success?

61

- What worked?

- Why was I able to achieve what I did?

Now take time to read over your answers to the second question—your disappointments and failures.

- What didn't work, and why?

- What would have worked better?

- What's the lesson?

- Have I learned it yet?

- Is there evidence to prove that I've learned it? What is it?

As you think back over your last year, there are lessons you've learned and others you *could* learn, given what happened. First find the ones you've already learned—the ones for which there's evidence that you've absorbed this lesson and moved on. Don't be too hard on yourself—if you *think* you've learned it, you have. It's important to capture it now so you can remember it and avoid having to learn it all over again.

Then there are the potential lessons. If only you'd done it differently. If only you'd not done it at all. If only you'd done it a better way. What advice do you have for yourself? It's time to move beyond guilt and recrimination, to let yourself off the hook. Assess what you did and how you want to do it next time.

Answering Question Three gives you a big opportunity—to learn, to change, to take on the challenges and make the moves you've been wanting to make. What would you have to do differently next time in order to have a better chance of success? What would it take?

■ **When we take the time to think, we know what we need to do and what we need to do differently. You <u>know</u> your most important lessons. Write them down.**

As you begin answering this third question, it's necessary to think more deeply about who you are and how you operate. This kind of thinking is beyond the thoughts that just pop up spontaneously. Make your brain work; sweep away the fog and find the answers. Trigger your mind with questions such as:

• What changes do I need to make in the way I operate?

• How can I do things differently?

• What advice do I have for myself?

• Do I need more discipline?

• Have I been as honest with myself and others as I need to be?

• Am I taking care of myself as well as I need to?

• Do I face difficult problems as quickly as I should?

• Have I let others support me? Do I listen to their advice and seriously consider taking it?

• Am I as supportive of others as I want to be?

• What lessons are there for me in my work? Am I a salesperson who needs to be more proactive? A manager who needs to pay more attention to what others have to say? A leader who could provide more direction or inspiration?

- Do I say "thank you" often enough?

## What Difference Would It Make?

One of the greatest motivations to learn our lessons is to imagine the difference it would make to those around us if we did. In fact, sometimes our desire to help others can strengthen our resolve to change our behavior.

But too often the lessons *others* need to learn are more obvious to us. Think about people you know and lessons you'd like them to learn. It's not difficult to see how much easier and more successful their lives would be if only . . . The same is true for you.

So pretend you're somebody else and look at your life with a bit more distance. As you sit on the bank of your life's river, what do you see? What could you do to avoid more of the rocks and boulders? What do you do that slows you down or stops you? Look at all the areas of your life: family, work, money, health, friends. What do you see? Look at other aspects: spirituality, service to community, doing your best at work.

Avoid judging yourself; you can move beyond that now. Practice thinking in new and more objective ways. Keep imagining you are sitting in the corner of your own life, watching yourself: What do you see? What do you like about what you see? What do you wish you'd do differently?

Rewrite the future. You know that if you change just a few ways of behaving, you can radically improve your chances of success. Think about just one of the lessons on your list. If you learned that one lesson in the next year, what difference would it make to you? Take the time to visualize yourself acting in this new way. Think about the potential benefits. *If I learned that . . .*

Once you've learned a lesson and are demonstrating it in your life, you've given yourself a gift like no other. Nothing can take it away from you. Not another person, not a major recession, not getting fired—nothing.

# Life Is a Classroom

The past year of your own life is a source of invaluable information. It tells you more about having what you want than all the lectures, books, videos, and cassettes you can find.

Your own experience of the past year is full of hints about success, increasing income, building positive relationships, gaining the kind of recognition you seek, achieving contentment and fulfillment, and making the kind of difference you want to make. What does the information tell you about being the kind of person you want to be?

**In examining your own life, you find more good sense than you can use to help you to have more of what you want in your life.**

Some of the lessons are so simple it's embarrassing. Everyone knows them; we've heard about them from many sources—parents, teachers, preachers, bosses, friends, books. Even more embarrassing is the length of time we've waited to learn the lessons. When I think how many situations happened over and over again in the same way before I stopped making the same mistakes, it's as if instead of using good common sense I was following *these* rules:

- Avoid opening the bills and reconciling the checkbook.

- Put up with relationships in which I'm made to feel small in order to feed someone else's ego because I'm too afraid to leave.

- Listen to others' troubles and don't ask for equal air time.

- Work so hard that I don't have time to take care of myself.

- Do all the easy stuff and procrastinate about the actions that would move me toward my goals.

I could go on. Our lessons are all around us; if we want to have our best year yet, year after year, we must wake up and see them. Becoming more aware of the gems in our own experience is better than striking gold. That only happens once, but our lessons pay off again and again.

As you begin to identify these lessons, the soil in your garden becomes enriched. You're starting to fertilize your ground and make way for growth. Thinking about mistakes and what you want to do differently starts to change the climate in which you live.

Consider how we learn about anything—for example, gardening. We get our information from many sources: parents, neighbors, friends, gardening books. But the best source is gardeners—people who are good at what they do and have demonstrated expertise over the years. When I'm in a tough situation or facing a big challenge, I sometimes think about someone who might face this situation with competence, and ask myself, "How would he do this? How would she handle this challenge? What would he say now?"

Yet, at the end of the day, only when we go into action and learn our own lessons does the difference show up in our own lives. It's easiest to learn from ourselves. We know this information best. Some of our lessons are things we've been saying to ourselves many times over the years. *Why don't you . . . ? What did you say that for? Wouldn't it have been better to . . . ?* What annoys us most is when we hear friends giving us advice that's the same as we've been telling ourselves for years—but haven't heeded.

I've learned that I must use the information or continue to get the lecture over and over again. My friend Lew Epstein often says "If only our ears could hear what our lips are saying" to refer to those times when we hear ourselves spouting wisdom that we'd do well to listen to ourselves. "Everything that irritates us about others can lead us to an understanding of ourselves," said Carl Jung.

> ◈ **The knowledge is there within us. We have only to think about the advice we have for others and then have the humility to see if we're following it ourselves.**

As you move forward in answering this question, you're already changing your way of doing things. By consciously considering the lessons you have to learn, you've made your life into a classroom in which you can learn from your own mistakes and move on. Answering this question alone will make a big difference in your next year.

# Turning Your Lessons into
# Personal Guidelines

If you haven't started your list, do it now. Write down all the lessons you can think of. Before you go on to the next step, make sure your list is complete and contains most of what you've thought as you've read through this chapter.

Now review the list. Think about each lesson and the difference it could make to you. Consider the changes you know you want to make now. Which ones could contribute the *most* to your success in making these things happen?

The next step is to choose your top three lessons, the ones that, if followed in the next year of your life, could make the most difference to you and to those around you. Give this some time and choose the ones that are best for you right now. You may be drawn to them instinctively, taking very little time. If so, trust your intuition and go with it.

I'm not suggesting that you forget the rest of the lessons on the list, but I hope you'll have a few good years after the next one to work on them. One of the key things I've learned in working with people is that it's necessary to focus, focus, focus. When you've finished your Best Year Yet process and you're back in the stream of life again, there will be only so much you can remember from this experience. Make it easy for yourself and give yourself every chance to win. Choose just three lessons for next year.

Once you've selected your three, turn them into instructions to follow over the next year. Take time to get the words just right. Each one should be as short and as clearly and powerfully stated as possible. Start with verbs and make the statements punchy. Tell yourself what *to do* rather than what *not to do*—in other words, express them as positively as you can. It's difficult for you to know what *to* do when the instruction is *not* to do something. However, if you feel the lesson must start with a word like "Don't" or "Stop" in order for you to remember it, state it that way.

These three lessons are your personal guidelines for the next year of your life. You've already made a big step toward enriching the soil in which you'll plant your goals for next year. Take a minute to imagine how different next year could be for you if you followed these lessons.

# Experiences

I call one of my personal guidelines "Face the music." By this I mean that I will confront troublesome issues and relationships. I stop avoiding doing what needs to be done and pretending that everything's fine.

For years I would find myself in tough situations and difficult relationships and yet do nothing. Nothing except practice angry internal conversations between myself and the other person, as I drove down the road or in the middle of the night or as I was making dinner, letting the bitterness build up and working myself up to the boiling point. By the time something had to be done, it was too late to do it well. I was so filled with emotion and resentment—my side of the story—that I usually made a mess of it.

Gradually I'm learning to wake up and notice when something isn't right and then take action right away. I book the time with myself to think it through, come up with possible solutions, understand how the other person might think and feel, and decide what to do and how to talk it over. Every time I succeed, the fog lifts and I'm again free and strong. And I've discovered that continuing to avoid difficult issues is harder than dealing with them.

Another guideline is "Use a coach to support me to do what I know to do." I've been a professional coach to others for over twenty years, and too often I make the mistake of not having a mentor myself. It's a dangerous trap, because I'm much more apt to do what I know works if I sit down and work with someone else, making a plan for myself, promising to carry it out, and then meeting for a progress check in a month's time.

Recently I've begun using a coach again and it's made all the difference. The last year was definitely my best year ever, and my coach was useful in keeping me on track as well as being a good listener during the rough times when I needed to make important decisions.

One guideline I'm proud to say I've practiced for years is "Do the tough stuff first." You've most likely heard as I have that only 20 percent of what there is to do really makes a difference, but knowing this and doing that 20 percent are not the same. How easy it is to make the cup of coffee, return nonurgent phone calls, chat with a friend or colleague, and so on, rather than tackle the one or two tasks that would make the most difference.

More and more often I just take myself to the top of the list and do that item first. My motivation is really a selfish one: As soon as that one is finished, I feel free, and the rest of the day is easy. Sometimes it's a scary phone call; more often a report, a letter, or a set of notes to write. Maybe the tax return or reconciling the bank statement. Whatever it is and whether it takes five minutes or five hours, I've found it works to do it first. I'm not operating at 100 percent on this, but I rarely let anyone down the way I used to do, and I believe this is one of my smartest guidelines for success.

Much of what I've learned about the value of identifying lessons has come from my work with clients. They've made the most progress through the process of taking responsibility for their own learning. They are their own best source of wisdom and advice, even though it's not always easy to follow.

When my colleagues and I are consulting in a business, we often work with teams of people who are working together to lead and manage the company. We start by carrying out an initial private interview with each executive to get his or her views on what's happening, how things are working, and what issues need to be resolved. Almost without exception, they are quite clear—including stories and tales to illustrate—about where the problems lie and which people need to change. However, it seems we're always talking to the innocent party. It's so easy to get out the blame gun and point it away from us. However, when asked what they could do or do differently to resolve the issue, the conversation changes and most are willing to identify steps they could take to make positive change in the business.

Questions are a coach's most powerful tool. People have inspired me by their answers and by their willingness to own up to mistakes. When they get in trouble, it's rarely because of their doubt about what to do. They do know the answers and the lessons they need to learn. The challenge is doing what they know to do. Yet their courage is inspiring—they are willing to see the problem, admit their part in it, and think about what to do to make things work.

So in order to stimulate your thinking, the following are some examples of guidelines used by family, friends, and clients:

- Put my family first.

- Ask for help when I need it.

- Only stay in relationships in which I feel good about myself.

- Relax.

- Do what I know to do.

- Face the music.

- Take the fun option.

- Take care of myself so I can take care of others.

- Do first things first.

- Be healthy.

- Let go, let God.

- Set aside time for myself and my husband.

- Enjoy the good in life.

# How Do I Limit Myself, and How Can I Stop?

*Life is a self-fulfilling prophecy.*

## How Do I Limit Myself?

Until I was thirty-three years old, I didn't realize how much I was limiting myself. If you'd asked me this question before that time, I might have said, "Yeah, maybe a little," but I hadn't begun to realize how much I limited myself or how I did it. I was much more aware of how situations and people around me were holding me back and how I had no choices, given my circumstances.

But I must have been getting in my own way, because once I started to become more conscious about my limiting behaviors, things started to change. It was then that I got out of the backseat of my life (thanks to a great teacher and the support of many important friends). Before then I rarely felt I was the source of my own experience or what happened to me—I was just a sleepy passenger in my life.

I was coping all right, but I felt generally frustrated, that something was missing. I was a disappointment to myself, lacking any awareness of how I had come to be that way or what I could do to make things different. At the rate I was going, I would never reach the place I'd hoped to go when I was younger, when I'd felt I had something to offer and could make a difference with my life.

I'd become an expert at explaining away situations and circumstances, living in silent sacrifice but for the most part not conscious of what I was doing. I was a good person but I had many unexpressed and unfulfilled longings. I'd come as far as I had only because I'd inherited a strong will and a good mind from both my parents.

When my journey of self-discovery began, I was shocked to find that my life up to then was just as *I* had created it. Instead of being a victim, I had shaped it by *my* thoughts and *my* actions. For instance, my relationships with my parents were a perfect reflection of my unexamined perceptions and attitudes about them. Until I woke up, my basic pursuit was to *make sure I don't grow up to be like my parents!*—an attitude that kept me from appreciating how much I *am* like them and what a gift they are to me.

I now began to appreciate that if I had made my life the way it was so far, I had the tools to make it even better. But the first step was to discover how I had been limiting myself—and I invite you now to do the same.

 **In order to have your best year yet, you must discover how you limit yourself and take responsibility for what's happened so far.**

Of course, you're close to this way of thinking or you wouldn't be reading this book, but the habit of thinking of ourselves as victims rather than as the ones responsible for ourselves is a strong one for most of us. A deep level of personal learning is available to you as you find out more about the context in which you're living your life and how it holds you back. In doing so, you discover the true meaning of Socrates' epigram "The unexamined life is not worth living." The rewards of this particular process are beyond your imagination.

The following questions are designed to help you to discover your limiting beliefs and the behaviors that result. As before, ask yourself the question and let your inner voice respond. The answers are already there; you don't have to think to find them.

## 1. How do I limit myself?

As you begin to answer this question, you may come up with all kinds of answers. Write them all down.

_____

_____

_____

_____

_____

_____

_____

_____

Here are some answers given by others:

- I don't take time to think about what's really important to me.

- I'm lazy.

- I believe what some other people say about me—their opinions carry more weight with me than my own.

- When I'm really attracted to someone, I don't do anything about it.

- I don't stand up for myself.

- I don't follow through on what I say I'm going to do—I let myself down time after time.

- I never ask for a raise, just wait to see what they give me.

- I spend more money than I make.

## 2. What has this cost me?

Although you're probably quite aware of some of the costs already, take some time to confront the true costs of your answers to the question above. Dig to the bottom. Doing so begins to loosen the grip of your past and how you think about yourself and what's possible.

_____

_____

_____

_____

_____

_____

_____

_____

Sample answers:

- A lot of money.

- A feeling that I've not made the best of the gifts given me.

- Relationships with people who matter to me.

- A husband who respects me and whom I respect.

- Fulfillment and contentment.

- Self-respect.

- My health.

You may notice that some of your answers to this question are reminiscent of the disappointments you listed in response to Question Two. This is fine—use the knowledge to reinforce your awareness of the connection between your thinking and your results.

## 3. In what ways have I benefited from limiting myself?

What? you say. How could *I* have benefited? The reason for asking this question is that we usually keep our limitations around because there's something in it for us. We're getting some reward from limiting ourselves and we're afraid we'd have to give it up in order to move on. At some level we know this and we hold on to our limitations so we don't lose their perceived benefits.

 **There is power in owning up to these hidden thoughts and attitudes, and thus beginning to separate yourself from them.**

It's especially important here just to ask yourself the question and write the answers that occur to you, whatever they are. Don't question your mental process—record your thoughts as you capture them, and avoid the temptation to edit the answers as they pop into your awareness. The true meaning of your thoughts will become more clear after you think about what you've written.

_____

_____

_____

_____

_____

_____

_____

_____

_____

Sample answers:

- An easy life.

- Not having much expected of me so I don't have to work so hard.

- I can live in ignorance and not have to face up to all of it.

- Making sure people like me and approve of me.

- A husband (anyone) to blame it all on.

- I always have the handy excuse that I could do better if I really tried.

- Keep the peace—don't rock the boat!

## 4. Am I *willing* to stop limiting myself?

The answer here is a simple yes or no. But it's obviously an important question. Don't worry about whether you think you're able or how you're going to go about it. Just ask yourself, "If I knew how, would I be willing to stop limiting myself?"

☐ Yes!      ☐ No.

If you haven't answered the four questions above,

### S T O P !

and go back and do so now. In order to connect fully with the important information that follows, it's essential that you be fully involved in this process.

How Do I Limit Myself, and How Can I Stop?    79

Once we're willing to become more aware of how we limit ourselves with our negative thoughts and beliefs, we're able to start seeing our past and its effect on us in a new light. One of my areas of greatest pain and unhappiness has been my relationships with men. When I started to dig into my attitudes and perceptions, I remembered an incident when I was a teenager. As you read this story from my past, notice how I limited myself by my thoughts alone!

A big school dance was announced, and this time the girls were to invite the boys rather than waiting to be asked. I'd had my eye on a football player named Mike for a long time, and this was my chance. But it wasn't easy. Every morning I'd wake up convinced today was the day I was going to ask him, planning how to bump into him while going over and over what to say. But day after day I lost my nerve.

Finally, time was short and I had to do it. I walked over to him, looked up and said, "Would you like to go to the dance with me?" His answer: "No, I don't think so. Sorry." What pain. I remember slinking down the school hallway, promising myself, "I'll never let that happen to me again!" Now that I knew I wasn't good enough to go out with Mike, I knew I wasn't good enough, period. *I'll stay in hiding and see if anyone finds me. But I'm never going to get caught letting someone know I care. No one's going to make the mistake of thinking I presume to be good enough to have one of the good ones.* I now knew my place.

From that point forward, I lived in the past, dragging Mike along with me. Every time I met a new man, he met me—and Mike. Although I was hopeful, I still thought of myself as reject material. The more I liked a man, the more uncomfortable I was and the more I stayed in hiding, scripting every remark and every move. Mike took center stage and I stayed in the wings. I had limited myself by one two-minute experience and the decisions I made about myself as a result. My relationships with men were shaped by my firm perception that I'd be lucky to have anyone, let alone one I really want.

It wasn't until I examined this way of thinking—the context for my relationships with men—that I could see its hold over me and what it had cost me over the years. Over and over again I settled for less than I wanted. In a period of self-examination such as the one shaped by Question Four, I shifted to a new way of thinking expressed by the statement "I can have any man I want!"

No sooner had I written this for the first time than I screamed at myself, "How unrealistic! Who am I kidding? What a laugh. Get serious." This is a typical reaction when we start to shift our fundamental limiting beliefs about ourselves. All our thoughts argue for our limitations. Our small mind is threatened. But I began to think in a new way about shifting the way I thought about myself and men. I took this seriously and began to see the possibility that "I can have any man I want" was more authentic than "I'd be lucky to have anybody."

Shifting from this limiting perception to an empowering perception was the finest gift I'd ever given myself. Within several months of making this shift, I met my Tim, and I'm now married to a man whom I respect and love deeply, a man who is way beyond anything I ever thought was possible for me. But before I examined my self-defeating notions about men, he would have been way too good for me and I'd never have considered he might be remotely interested in me.

This may sound like an extravagant claim. Of course, we may have met, fallen in love, and been just as happy without this profound shift in my perception, but you'll never convince me!

# What You Focus on Is What You Get

I hope you're able to see that as long as I thought of myself as a rejected woman, I was bound to be disappointed in love. The results in our lives are a perfect match for our expectations. So often we get what we predict we'll get. But it works both ways—negatively and positively. That's the magic. Wherever you have a positive focus in your life, you're probably getting good results. However, for the purpose of this exercise, we're considering the negative aspects because that's where you'll find the secrets to moving to the next level of your personal effectiveness and power.

What are you focusing on now? What grabs your attention? I don't mean your coffee cup or this page in the book, but rather your inner thoughts and attitudes. The purpose of the fourth Best Year Yet question is to help you discover your fundamental limiting perceptions about yourself and your life—ways of thinking and feeling that stop you from achieving what's really possible.

**The first step is to realize the connection between your limiting thoughts and the areas of your life in which your results are disappointing. Only then can you shift to a new way of thinking that empowers you to have the results you want.**

But first look at the examples below, gathered from many people who thought about the connection between their inner focus and the results they were achieving.

| WHAT DO I FOCUS ON? | WHAT DO I GET? |
|---|---|
| My wide hips. | No dates. |
| Fear of failure in business. | Cash-flow crises. |
| Anger at not being treated fairly. | Not being treated fairly. |
| Resentment with my husband's preoccupation with business. | He pays little attention to me. |
| How little time I have. | Not enough time—being behind in everything and out of control. |

What are you thinking and worrying about? What are you *really* predicting for yourself: success or failure? Are you focusing on your fears or your strengths? Your doubts or your goals? Think about it—check out the premise that *what you focus on is what you get*. What's true for you? Don't believe a word I say unless it matches your experience.

Ask yourself, "What am I focusing on now?" Make a list of these thoughts and feelings down the left side of a piece of paper. Stop and do that now.

Then begin to think about what you're getting as a result of the focus of your thoughts and feelings. Look at the answers on the left and think about what's happening in your life. Is it possible that your relationships are a mirror of what you predict and expect? Is your career a reflection of your expectations? Ever catch yourself saying to yourself, "See!" or "I'm not surprised!"? But this pursuit to be right rarely brings us the results we seek.

How are your thoughts and feelings related to what you're getting? Is there a link between your mental and emotional focus and what you're achieving in your life? Where do your thoughts and feelings lead you? Beside each item you've listed, write the actual results you have in this area of your life.

◆ **When we take responsibility for our capacity for positive change, we can control and guide our intelligence and our feelings and point them toward the results we want. As this happens, we are drawn toward our goals as if by a magnet.**

When I took my focus away from my teenage rejection and focused on what I wanted—*a lifelong relationship with a man I love and respect*—that's what I attracted into my life.

The purpose of this line of questioning is to discover what's running your life—you or your limitations. Until you're aware of where you are now, you can't change direction. Unless you're aware of something, you can't change it.

# The Fried Egg

The model I use to illustrate this area is now called the Fried Egg, thanks to a client who said that's what it looked like to him. It's actually a cross-section of our mental and emotional makeup—a psychological model to enable us to understand ourselves a bit better. It may at first be difficult to grasp because it not only relates to our basic relationship with ourselves but also begins to describe how the mind works. Stay with it, as this information is *the bottom line for making permanent lasting change.*

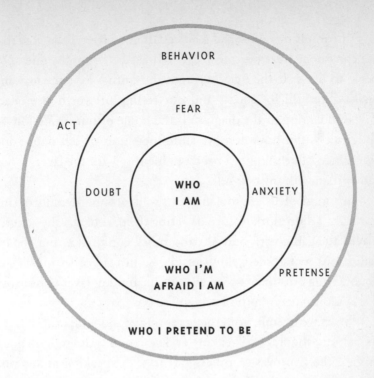

At the center of each of us—the circle in the middle of the diagram—is an experience of ourselves and our values; for most of us what we call our heart or soul: "Who I am." The part that never changes.

Over time, more and more of this central core of inner strength can become hidden beneath a layer of fear, anxiety, doubt, and years of habitual behavior that no longer represents who we are. Our failures are pointed out to us by well-meaning parents and teachers in a way that focuses on the middle ring more than the center: Others speak to us in a way that makes us feel that there is something wrong with *us* rather than with our behavior or performance. We then identify with "Who I'm afraid I am" and forget who we really are.

How Do I Limit Myself, and How Can I Stop?     85

The resulting doubt and fear lead us away from behaviors that are consistent with our most deeply held beliefs and values. We begin to live as if the middle ring is the truth—as if the fear and anxiety are well founded—and our feeling of worth is eroded. The middle ring of the diagram is the home of our limitations— the space within us where we store memories of self-doubt and fear. Once Mike said no, I began to identify with the layer of fear rather than with my true self.

But most of us are too smart to walk around demonstrating our fears. I didn't lurk in corners acting the part of the shy reject! I played the game with bravado and mock confidence, but the facade didn't match the feelings inside. So instead of letting all our doubts hang out for all to see, we pile on another layer to hide our doubt and anxiety: "Who I pretend to be."

When we operate from the outer ring or more superficial level, we fall into the trap of speaking and acting in order to look good or gain the approval of others rather than speaking and acting honestly in ways that are consistent with what we want and what we value. We also lose touch with the center and begin to think that the real us is the middle ring: *Thank God they don't know how bad I am!* This is what one client calls the Impostor Syndrome.

**Discovering how we limit ourselves uncovers the doubts and fears and starts the process of erasing the effects they have on us.**

If you can move your awareness back to the center, to your inherent strength and power, you will get back in touch with who you are. You will stop limiting yourself and start again to express yourself from the center, through the layer of ritual doubts and fears. It takes practice, but the years of doubt and fear begin to dissolve. Mike became a memory, but my painful experience with him (and the self-doubt I once created) no longer guides my relationships with men.

# How Can I Stop?

So, how do we move beyond our self-defeating behaviors and shift our ways of thinking and feeling about ourselves so we stay in touch with our strength and value? Before you discover *what* you want in the next year of your life, take time to create the mental and emotional environment in which you can succeed.

A transformation occurs when you place yourself at the center of your life, creating your world rather than letting circumstances dictate your success. You use your intelligence and your power to create a new reality for yourself. The process is one of shifting from a limiting to an empowering perception of yourself and the world in which you live. You shift from a false reality to an authentic reality.

We're now ready to talk about the most powerful tool for personal transformation: the paradigm shift. A paradigm is a way of seeing and thinking about yourself, someone else, an aspect of your life—anything. Think of a paradigm as a set of glasses through which you see everything around you, including yourself. Except that you're not aware that the glasses are there—you think you're seeing things as they really are.

After I was turned down for the dance, my paradigm for my

relationships with men was: "I'd be lucky to have anyone, let alone someone I really want."

From that moment I lived inside that assumption. That was my reality, the truth for me. I was not aware of any other way of acting or thinking about the subject of men, even though there was evidence that men were attracted to me.

> **Our limiting paradigms are not corrected by the facts. We believe we're right and no external piece of data can change our minds.**

I've known hundreds of successful people whose personal paradigms were still limiting—no level of achievement, wealth, or recognition would shift their perception of themselves. Once a limiting paradigm is in place, we must use our intelligence and our heart to shift to a more empowering one. If we do not think of ourselves as successful or worthy, no achievement or level of recognition will shift this for us. It is an inside-out job!

Can you remember thinking that as soon as you earned $x$ amount of money, your troubles would be over? Were they? Have you ever told yourself that if only you could live with someone, you'd be happy? Was it enough?

When we make this fundamental shift in perception, we are able to stop looking at the future with eyes of fear. "As a man thinketh in his heart, so he becomes," says the Bible. Learn to think about your strengths and your value.

You are the product of your thoughts and feelings. To change the results, change the way you think. Instead of investing your intelligence and energy in beliefs with negative outcomes, switch your focus to beliefs that lead where you want to go.

⬙ **Circumstances don't create our reality,**

**our happiness, our contentment, or our**

**fulfillment. That's _our_ job.**

We each have many limiting paradigms, a sophisticated set of thoughts, excuses, defenses—our bottom-line reasons for failing. We put them in charge and we follow their lead—until we wake up. And when we do, the choice between reasons and results is clear. In Deepak Chopra's book *Ageless Body, Timeless Mind,* he describes the paradigm of aging, a way of thinking that leads to degeneration and decay. He lets us know that we human beings have the intelligence and the capacity to shift to a paradigm of agelessness:

> *There is no biochemistry outside awareness; every cell in your body is totally aware of how you think and feel about yourself. Once you accept that fact, the whole illusion of being victimized by a mindless, randomly degenerating body falls away.*

The first step in your transformation is to discover your limiting paradigms. How do you think in ways that hold you back? What ritual doubts and fears shape your self-image? Answer the following questions to find your limiting beliefs.

# In what areas of my life am I not achieving what I want?

_____

_____

_____

_____

_____

_____

Answer this first question quickly—just a list of bulleted points such as:

• Relationships with women/men.

• Balance between work and play.

• Making money.

• Creativity.

• Keeping fit.

Now consider these aspects of your life and how you think and talk about yourself as a result of these failures. What do you say about yourself to explain these circumstances? What do you say to yourself about yourself? What do you say about yourself to others? Push yourself to find out how you talk about yourself. In these answers you start to discover your own limiting paradigms.

# What do I say about myself to explain these failures?

_____

_____

_____

_____

_____

_____

Your answers might sound like some of these:

- No matter how hard I try, I'll never make it.

- I haven't got what it takes.

- Because I didn't go to college, I'm not smart enough.

- I'm too old—it's too late.

- I'm too busy—too much to do already!

- I don't deserve it.

- I'm lucky to have what I have now.

- I've got no choice.

- I'm probably earning more than I deserve now—hope I'm not found out!

Remembering the Fried Egg model, think of your answers as the inhabitants of your middle ring. With these limiting paradigms in charge, where will they lead you? What you focus on is what you get, and paradigms create our fundamental focus in life. They dictate the size of our success, the quality of our relationships, and the depth of our fulfillment. With these paradigms in charge, the results will be disappointing. Becoming more aware of them by writing them down begins to loosen their grip and starts to lessen their power over you.

We unknowingly empower these beliefs with our intelligence and then get results that are consistent with these limiting beliefs.

Once you feel your list is complete, at least for now, circle the answers that have the strongest influence on you. Which ones do you consider to be the truth? Which one do you *really* buy into? Work with one of these as we move on to the technology of shifting paradigms.


# Paradigm Shifts

Finding your limiting paradigms is a giant step in awareness.

For much of my life money was a problem. No matter what I did, I spent more than I earned and was always getting into trouble. Bills and bank statements hid in the desk drawers unopened, and often it took the threat of legal action to push me into a late-night panic of self-recrimination and scurrying to get my act together, yet again.

A couple of times I took out a credit consolidation loan from the bank, paid off my credit cards and my bills, and wiped the slate clean. But I couldn't resist the temptation of spending up to the credit card limits again. I can't remember how many times this happened, but too many.

Nothing I did seemed to end the hopeless cycle because my actions were driven by a hidden limiting paradigm: "I want more money, but I'll never make more than I'm making now—it's all I'm worth!" As long as I thought in this way, the results were the same, no matter what I tried to do differently. I was pulled by an invisible magnet back into the same pit.

But once I started to examine the limiting ways I was thinking and feeling about money, the underlying paradigm became obvious to me. At a young age, I'd made a bunch of rules and decisions about money, but they'd hid behind the cobwebs of my consciousness and I didn't know they were there. The results in my life should have given me a clue, but I didn't know how to discover their true meaning. Once I started to examine the way I thought about money, I found I'd made two fundamental rules that shaped my limiting paradigm about money and dictated the financial results I achieved:

- It's not all right to make more money than the man you're with.

- It's not fair to make a lot of money when people are starving.

And then there were the usual ones that nevertheless had a strong influence on me:

- Money is the root of all evil.

- I'm not the kind of person to make a lot of money.

- Money is scarce—there's only so much to go around.

- If I made a lot of money, I'd be horrible and greedy.

- I don't have as much talent as people who make a lot of money.

When I looked at my list to see which were the most influential for me, it was the one about people starving. I'd been convinced for so long that playing the money game would be a sellout of my soul. How could I think about changing that idea? It was sinful to be so selfish.

But as I followed the thought, I realized that this paradigm of scarcity and unworthiness kept *me* poor as well as others. What could my poverty contribute to them? What could I do for them when I couldn't even pay my own bills? It was then that I realized that transforming my relationship with money was really a transformation in self-worth. I imagined that if I could get to the bottom of this one and start earning the kind of money I really wanted and secretly thought I deserved, I'd be in a stronger position—both within myself and within my wallet—to give to others. I wrote a new empowering paradigm for money in my life: "Money is abundant and flows spontaneously in life. Money allows me to express myself fully and contribute generously." This has been a source of inspiration and power to me over the past twenty years. My income now is many times what it was then, and I give more to others each year than my total annual earnings back then. And it started by my answering Question Four.

## A New Empowering Paradigm for a New Year

### FOUR STEPS TO SHIFTING A PARADIGM

1. Discover your limiting paradigm.

2. Think about what's holding it in place, such as limiting thoughts, feelings, and perceived benefits.

3. Create a new, empowering paradigm.

4. Learn the art of transformation. Increase your awareness and shift to your new paradigm whenever you become ensnared by your old limiting paradigm.

We've been through the first two steps of shifting paradigms. If you haven't already done so, choose the limiting paradigm you're going to be shifting in order to generate your best year yet.

**You don't need to change everything at once— start by discovering one of your strongest limiting paradigms.**

Now that you've completed the first two steps of shifting a paradigm, you can go to work creating a new way of perceiving and thinking that leads you to the results and relationships you want for yourself in the next year of your life.

Transformation is a fundamental change in the way you relate to who you are, what you do, and what you have in your life. When you create a shift in a limiting paradigm, you take charge of your life.

Whether limiting or empowering, the dynamic of paradigms is the same. Each is represented by a statement that encapsulates our perceptions and what we believe. We think the statement is right and we use all our resources to create that reality—and it works. We prove the truth of that perception over and over again—in our thinking, feelings, actions, behavior, results, relationships—

everywhere. So you already have the ability to give truth to a paradigm—just shift to one that gives you a better return on your investment.

 **Once you understand and accept the dynamic of the self-fulfilling paradigm, you can use it to your advantage.**

To write a new paradigm, look at your current limiting paradigm. What statement would describe a new perception that could destroy the old one? As you look at the following examples of limiting and empowering paradigms, you may feel that the empowering paradigms are too positive or simplistic. Move past that thought. Think about your limiting paradigm and what you'd like to make happen instead.

| LIMITING PARADIGM | EMPOWERING PARADIGM |
|---|---|
| I'm lucky to have anybody. | I can have anyone I want. |
| I know best. | I enjoy learning from others and succeed far more quickly with their support. |
| I want more money but I'm not worth any more than I'm making now. | Money is abundant and flows spontaneously in my life. |

| I can't do what I really want to do. | I empower myself to have what I want. |
| I'm not good enough. | I have much to offer and I enjoy finding places to give. |

Don't put limits on what you want to create for yourself. Decide what you want and write a statement that expresses it clearly. How do you do that? You make it up!

Your statement should express precisely what you want for yourself. When you first write it, it may exist only on the intellectual level. You have yet to experience its truth and you probably don't own it mentally or emotionally. But if it's a stretch for you to think in the way your new paradigm suggests, you're on the right track.

Notice the way in which the new paradigms above are worded. Each meets the following criteria for an empowering paradigm:

- Personal

- Present tense

- Positive

- Powerfully stated

- Pointing to an exciting new possibility

Once you have written your statement, make sure it's exactly right for you. Where does your new paradigm lead you? Exactly what results will you have when it comes true? Make sure the words express *precisely* the new reality you want to create.

**Remember: our paradigms create our results and our relationships.**

Go beyond reasonableness and ordinary rationale. Make a quantum leap in your thinking. Allow yourself to think seriously about new possibilities and become enthusiastic about what could happen in your life. Expect a few miracles. Now that you have a new paradigm, you've given your garden its best dose of fertilizer. Imagine what's going to happen to goals planted in soil nourished by this paradigm. Albert Einstein thought that "imagination is more important than knowledge."

 **It's time to stand apart from your limiting thoughts and feelings and replace them with ones that lead you in the direction you want to go.**

Remember, this is the *truth* about you; it's not just positive thinking. As you read it, remind yourself, "This is a statement about who I am." Your limiting paradigm is a reflection of the middle ring—the doubts and fears. A lie. Your new paradigm is a statement of truth about you. You are moving on from the limited historical view of yourself and getting back in touch with your true self. Make sure that your new paradigm empowers you to achieve the goals you want for yourself in your best year yet.

When we are the victim of a limiting paradigm, we live an

unexamined, unconscious life. If we'd stop to think, we would see that our jumbled view of things was getting us nowhere. Often our limiting paradigm is a paradox—so our internal messages are not only negative, they are conflicting. Look at the cartoon below. The thoughts on the right side of the head are pulling in the direction of having *more* money. The thoughts on the left side of the head are pulling in the opposite direction: toward all the reasons why this person *can't* have more. As we know from physics, when two forces are pulling in equal and opposite directions, there is inertia; *we don't go anywhere.* Sound familiar?

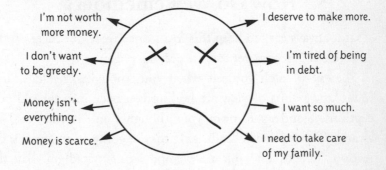

However, once we have an empowering paradigm—a focus we have consciously constructed to bring us what we want—we have one focus toward which to direct our intention and awareness.

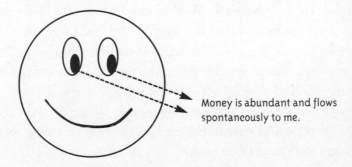

All our intellect and emotions are pointed in the same direction. In the cartoon above there's no dilution of energy or confusion of focus. While the person in the first picture seems at best to be headed round and round in circles, the second person is in the driver's seat and knows where he or she is going. When you operate in this way, there is the possibility of a new reality based on personal truth, and you have a strong motivation to keep your eye on the road that leads you where you want to go.

## How Do We Remember?

It's not always easy to keep this focus once we're out there on the road to our best year yet and life gets busy again.

Learn to catch yourself when your thoughts, feelings, attitudes, and points of view are leading you back into the old perceptions. Stand apart from your thoughts and feelings and be aware of where they're leading. If they're going in the wrong direction, refocus on your new empowering paradigm. Say the words to yourself. Consciously shift the way you direct your intelligence and the investment of your emotions and intentions.

One of my most effective mental tricks is to envision my head as a bird cage. On one side of my head is the entrance, on the other the exit. I see my thoughts as birds who enter the bird cage. If they are limiting thoughts that don't lead where I want to go, I make sure the exit is open and imagine these thoughts flying right back out again and disappearing into the air. I do my best to avoid the temptation of inviting a bird to dinner, agreeing with what he says, and thus feeding him until he gets so fat he can't get out again. Then I could start to believe that the bird's limiting message is the truth, and I'd be hooked.

Many people write their new empowering paradigms on bits of paper and stick them around in spots where the words grab their attention, for example on the bathroom mirror or the front of the refrigerator. I once learned to look up every word of a new personal paradigm in the dictionary to reach a new level of understanding and appreciation for the new paradigm and its underlying intention.

◈ **Be creative in your paradigms. Direct your life force and your awareness toward the perception that is most accurate and empowering for you.**

Above all, be aware of how you speak about yourself to others. While I'm not suggesting that you indulge in parrotlike iterations of your new paradigm at every opportunity, speak in ways that support your new sense of yourself. For instance, while I didn't talk with people about my new money paradigm, I did let people know at appropriate moments that money was no longer a problem for me.

To have your best year yet, you must not only change what you do but how you think and feel. Changing either your external behavior or your mental and emotional environment alone is not enough. Positive, lasting change comes from moving both at once.

Learning the science and art of the paradigm shift is life's greatest gift. Learning to design and implement your new paradigm is the secret to taking charge of your own life rather than being guided by the invisible hand of a limiting paradigm. What could be better?

# What Are My Personal Values?

*It is not enough to possess virtue as if it were an art.*
*It should be practiced.*

MARCUS TULLIUS CICERO

## What's Driving You?

The promise of this book is to put you back in the driver's seat of your life. Becoming more aware of your personal values helps you to understand what really motivates you. Why, for example, do you pick up books like this? What are you looking for and why?

What drives most of us is the ambition to improve the quality of our lives while being true to ourselves and what's really important to us. Although we may not be conscious of these basic motivations as we live day to day, these hidden drives are the strongest in our lives. The more conscious we are of them, the more we empower ourselves to make the necessary changes in our lives.

When you examine the underlying drive for each of your conscious goals, you'll find out what really gets you out of bed in the morning. The more aware you are of this dynamic, the more genuinely enthusiastic you'll be to throw the covers off and get going.

When I ask people about what they want, they usually respond by saying something like a promotion, a new car, a vacation, more income, a husband or wife, a child. But usually there's something lying behind these goals—a less obvious goal or objective.

We may think, for example, that we want a new car, but is it the *thing* itself or what it represents to us? Is it the way we'll feel when we drive the car—the experience of pleasure or ease in getting where we want to go? Or is it how others will think of us when they see us with the new car—the feeling of prestige or wealth? Or perhaps, with some cars, it's a sense of power we're really after. Once we uncover the real goal, we can focus on it as well as the original more tangible goal, and therefore have a better chance of getting what we truly want.

Perhaps one of your goals is to become more fit. Are you motivated by the moment you'll get your gold star from the doctor, or are you really pursuing greater energy or improved self-esteem? These intangibles are based on the personal value of *taking care of yourself*.

The fact that we're unaware of these hidden unconscious drivers is the reason we often don't feel satisfied when we finally achieve a goal. Ever had the experience of working as hard as you could for a long time to achieve a goal, only to feel let down when you finally reached it? Often it's not the achievement itself we're after but the experience we're hoping it will provide us when we do achieve it.

When I discovered that it wasn't more money itself I was after but the chance to express myself fully and contribute more generously, I had a major breakthrough in my ability to generate money.

I connected the goal with two strong personal values: *self-expression* and *contributing to others*. For example, if you have a family your desire for more money is possibly not the money itself but the chance to be true to your personal value of *loving my family*.

If your objective is a promotion at work, more money may be your tangible objective, but the desire for a greater sense of achievement and more recognition of who you are and what you're capable of could be your underlying and more intangible aim. The personal value of *self-expression* or *self-actualization* is more likely what keeps you going.

Underlying most of our tangible goals, like a home, a car, money, vacations, or clothes, are the intangible goals that bring us to a greater manifestation of our personal values. When we are aware of these values, we see a clearer picture of who we are and, more important, find the greater motivation to make change in our lives.

## Basic Life Pursuits

One of the biggest blocks on the road to full self-expression is the underlying assumption that we're *still* not good enough to be the kind of person we'd really like to be! This feeling springs from the limiting paradigm "What can I do to prove myself? To be good enough?" Our life pursuit of changing ourselves is often built on the lie that we're not good enough already and need to do something more before we can truly show who we are.

Where does this limiting paradigm lead us? We waste vast amounts of energy striving to prove ourselves, our worth, and our value. We look for approval more than results. And it's easy to fall into the trap of valuing others' opinions more than our own.

Years ago I got a good roasting from a colleague who accused me of being totally self-serving in my approach to my work. It took me months of soul-searching to come to my senses and realize that what she said was inaccurate and her assumptions were incorrect. I understood why she had attacked me but I knew her perception was not true. During this painful process I strengthened my commitment to live according to my personal values and to trust my motivation to contribute to others.

I've seen board executives in large companies who think and act as if they were still waiting to be given permission to take the ball and run with it. Instead of making the changes they've been longing to make once they rose to a position of leadership and influence, they still hold back, afraid to take the lead they've earned.

Use the model below to consider your own life pursuit. Is it characterized by the circle on the left or the one on the right? How are you investing your intelligence and your life force? If you see that you're engaged in Life Pursuit I, your awareness and your commitment to shift to Life Pursuit II are sufficient to make a fundamental difference in your life.

LIFE PURSUIT
I

LIFE PURSUIT
II

WHAT CAN I
DO TO PROVE
MYSELF?
TO BE GOOD
ENOUGH?

WHAT CAN I
DO WITH THE
GIFTS I
HAVE?

Sometimes it takes a bit of time to figure out what we're doing and which pursuit we're engaged in. When Tim and I were first married, we would sit at the dinner table in the evenings having our meal, sharing a bottle of wine, and talking over how the day had gone. He was starting a company and found himself in a position of leadership and total corporate responsibility for the first time in his life. Although it was what he'd always wanted, it was frightening and scary now that the time had come to make it happen.

Every time he faced another new challenge—making his first cash flow, making more sales, training new staff—he'd have another attack of self-doubt. He was open with me and let me know how he was feeling. Night after night I reassured him, reminding him of his strengths. After months I noticed a similarity in our conversations—they didn't seem to be making him feel any better. I realized I'd become part of the problem and was feeding into his paradigm of Life Pursuit I. We had to stop playing this game in order to help him empower himself. One night when he was sharing his doubts about himself, I said, "You know, maybe you're right. You might not have what it takes!" That was the end of that game.

This lifelong habit of insufficiency and unworthiness can be transformed into the healthier and more fulfilling Life Pursuit II, "What can I do with the gifts I have?"

Life Pursuit II is based on an empowering paradigm—one that places living up to one's values ahead of ego and survival. It is driven by values such as the desire to make things work, to support others, to make the best use of our gifts, and to keep our promises. Living in the context of this pursuit makes all the difference to our approach to life. There's no time to indulge in self-doubt and fear—there's too much to do.

Life Pursuit I is focused on personality and superficial self-improvement. When we're captured by this game, we're self-absorbed, inwardly focused, and, I believe, generally wasting our time trying to work out what's wrong with us. There are the breakthroughs and the realizations, but a person in this trap never changes their basic life story—there are new chapters perhaps, but always within the same overall theme: *I'm not good enough.*

One of my finest teachers worked hard to teach me this lesson. Once in a meeting he said to me, "You remind me of an orange tree straining to grow an orange." It took me weeks to figure out what he meant, but eventually I realized he was telling me that I was caught up in Life Pursuit I and that this was a waste of my time and energy. An orange tree grows oranges—it doesn't waste one molecule of energy worrying about whether it has what it takes. Sounds ridiculous, doesn't it?

But that's exactly what we do when we waste time in self-doubt and fear rather than focusing ourselves on what we can do right now with what we have. Imagine starting your day with the intention of discovering where you can use your talents. What difference would that make to you in your life? When I have seen people stand in their strengths and get on with it, it is truly inspiring.

I spent most of the first year of my marriage being upset and demanding more love from Tim. "Why are you so tired all the time?" "Why don't you help out more around the house?" "Why don't you ever get home when you say you will?" "Why don't you initiate some of our social engagements?" "Why don't you arrange the theater, the movies, our vacations . . ." and so on. In short, I was really asking him, "Why don't you love me more?" This was Life Pursuit I at its best: I was trying to get Tim to prove he loved me, time after time, so that I'd know *I* was good enough.

And then one day I woke up. Given that *I* wanted a loving relationship, I wasn't acting consistently with that value. In fact, I was doing just the opposite by creating an upsetting atmosphere of argument, complaint, justification, and anxiety. I was the one who was creating it. He wasn't complaining. I was.

I realized that if I wanted a loving relationship, it was up to me to make it that way. I knew I had the power. That was the good news: If I wanted it to be different, I had the power the change it. But then there was the bad news: It wasn't a question of whether I was *able* to do it; it was whether I was *willing* to take the leading role in making our relationship a loving one. It was whether I was willing to stop withholding my love while waiting for him to change. It was whether I could give up the "I will if you will" game.

What enabled me to change the way I was acting was the realization that I was not behaving in a way that was consistent with my values, with what I believed in. I was acting like a victim. I was *reacting* to my environment. I was expecting my husband to provide me with the relationship I wanted. Once I began to be the way I wanted the relationship to be—in a word, loving—the relationship moved from strength to strength. I switched to Life Pursuit II in my marriage. I found that *marriage is an opportunity to love,* not a place to prove that I'm okay or that *I'm* loved.

And guess what? Tim's been far more loving, supportive, romantic, helpful—all I wanted. But it was no accident. And it started with my being true to my value of loving.

Life Pursuit II is outwardly focused. It incorporates an awareness of our world and the people in it, a consciousness of the effects we have on people, problems, and circumstances. But this does not mean self-sacrifice for the sake of others. The first responsibility of any person engaged in Life Pursuit II is to take care of him- or herself.

# What's Most Important to You?

What really gets you out of bed in the morning? Why do you work so hard? What drives you to do what you do? Your automatic response may be that you have no choice—again, you are the victim of circumstances. But it's time to go beyond that level of awareness to find out what you're really up to.

*Who are you and what values do you want to demonstrate in your life?* Find the drive in you that's so strong it could motivate you to create a new kind of life for yourself. Take the time to discover the personal values that are strong enough to drive you to live from the new empowering paradigm you've created for yourself.

When we do this, we tell ourselves, "I've had enough! I'm good enough and I'm ready to get going." With this kind of determination, you can break through the self-doubt and pretense of the Fried Egg model and express yourself more fully in your life. You can move past your laziness, inertia, failures, excuses, and feeling of resignation, and move on to your best year yet.

You're not on an assembly line; you're a finished product. Turn it on and drive it!

# What Are Your Personal Values?

Your values are your personal principles or standards—your judgment of what's important or valuable in your life. Values are deeply held beliefs that live in the heart and soul of each of us. We want them to shape the way we work, make choices, and take care of our loved ones. They form the foundation of every human being.

As you define your personal values, beware of a potential limiting paradigm such as "I'm not a good person." This just gives you another excuse to fail, thereby proving to yourself either that you're not living up to your values or, worse, that you don't have admirable principles to begin with; another manifestation of Life Pursuit I.

Awareness of our personal values and our commitment to Life Pursuit II averts our attention from hidden, destructive, negative drivers, such as:

- resentment

- a need to get even

- a desire to generate sympathy

- the "I'll show them" syndrome

- martyrdom

- wanting to make others sorry for the way they treat you

One way of thinking about what's important in the grand scheme of things is to think about the end of your life. How do you want to be remembered? What do you want on your tombstone? What do you wish others to say about you as they stand around at your funeral? Above all, what do you want to be admired for?

When I've worked with people and led them through this process, the same personal values have surfaced over and over again. They are fundamental, undeniable, and hold true for all people. Common on people's lists would be values such as:

- integrity

- taking care of myself

- loving my family

- self-actualization

- making a difference

- keeping promises

- honesty

- trust

- peace of mind

- happiness

- compassion for others

- respect

- sense of accomplishment

- demonstrating my best

- expressing myself

Think about your personal mission and values. Ask yourself such questions as:

- What values represent who I am?

- What values do I want to demonstrate?

- What do I want to happen as a result of my interaction with others?

- What effect do I want to have on others?

# What Are My Personal Values?

Take time now to write down your own personal values.

_____

_____

_____

_____

_____

_____

_____

   The aim here is to clarify your values and strengthen your awareness of them in your heart and mind. Fundamental principles or values do not change. Whether you're demonstrating your belief in these values is another issue that you can address as you plan your next year—but don't doubt them.

 **If you remember instances when you weren't true to your values, think of them as times when you weren't being yourself. We all make mistakes— but we can learn from them and move on. That's life. As long as your roots are strong, you can grow again and again. That's the way of nature.**

# Beyond the Goodies

Living a life based on personal values takes us to a place in which we are motivated by more than the acquisition of goodies—our material world and its pleasures. There's nothing wrong with these, but they are milestones rather than the true reason for living. Don't get me wrong, I'm not an ascetic—far from it. But the purpose of my own goodies and the pleasure they bring is to nourish and replenish my spirit so I am better able to fulfill my mission in life. As an end in themselves, they don't provide satisfaction or fulfillment.

The decade of the 1980s has been called the age of greed—one in which so many got caught up in the "goodies game" for its own sake. We know of many people who, in the process, failed to live according to their fundamental life principles and were caught red-handed. Part of the value of these people's mistakes is to wake us up to what happens to those caught in the act of not being true to others or themselves.

Becoming more aware of your personal values and raising your consciousness about them is an invaluable step toward your best year yet. The process awakens your strongest drivers and your most natural motivations.

In truth, there's no hiding place for any of us. We're not invisible. We see others fully and they see us in the same way. When we speak and live our personal values, it's obvious. When we forget, the same is true. But when we become more conscious of our personal values, we can make sure that the person the world sees is someone we are proud of.

As you go along, catch yourself being true to yourself; appreciate yourself—it's a great motivator. One of my client friends carries out what he calls his "pillow check" each night before he goes to sleep. He reviews what happened during the day, when he lived in a way he was proud of, and times he could have done better.

Dare to be who you are. Break through the barrier of self-doubt and pretense to express your true self. Let yourself live more in line with your values. The first few steps as we come out of hiding can be frightening, but the sense of freedom and fulfillment is enormous.

# What Roles Do I Play in My Life?

*It often happens that I wake at night and begin to think about a
serious problem and decide I must tell the Pope about it. Then I
wake up completely and remember that I am the Pope.*

POPE JOHN XXIII

## Why Think About Roles?

Answering this question allows you to get an overall view of all
the aspects and responsibilities of your life. Stopping to think
about the various roles I play has always brought me back to sanity at times when I found myself wondering if I was getting anywhere or just wearing myself out.

**Looking at your life from the perspective of
the roles you play provides a sensible way of
integrating the various areas of your life while
placing yourself and your values at the center,
directing the show.**

117

There are many additional benefits to thinking of your life from the vantage point of the roles you play:

**1. It provides direction.** Whether I think of myself in my role as a mother or as a coach, I can create a timeless sense of myself and see the river of my life—where it's going and where I'd like it to go. I picture myself in the center, in control and able to guide myself in the direction in which I want to go while maintaining an awareness of my principles.

Thinking of your roles enables you to direct yourself and design your life with a meaning beyond that of just getting along. You create a continuum of values allowing you to strengthen your sense of self—your sense that you are the one who guides the playing of each role in your life. You move to a place beyond the illusion of thinking you have no choices.

**2. It places *who you are*—your values—at the center of your life.** As you make a connection between your roles and how you play them, you're able to consider how you would play each role to bring it in line with what's most important to you. This is a far more valid and validating way of measuring your success in life.

 **Awareness is everything. Just thinking about your roles and your values shifts the way you think about yourself and your life. It puts you in the driver's seat as nothing else can.**

I have often found self-improvement declarations confusing simply because I couldn't figure out how to follow suggestions such as "Stand up for yourself" or "Be more assertive" without feeling that I'd be selling out in some way or walking all over the people around me. When you focus on your roles and values, however, doubts and fears dissolve. You will find, for example, that the true expression of the personal value of "loving my family" makes it impossible *not* to assert yourself in your role as partner and parent.

**3. It makes Life Pursuit II the natural option.** As you think of your life from the viewpoint of the roles you play, you are naturally looking outward. It's difficult if not impossible to wallow in self-pity or indulge in self-doubt when your eyes and your awareness are focused outside yourself.

Think of a time when you helped a friend who was in trouble. Did you spend time wondering if you were able to do it, or did you just get on with it, giving it everything you had?

When you're conscious of your desire to play the role of friend and have a mental image of how you want that to look and be, it dissolves the need to prove yourself or waste your energy in needless approval seeking. The spotlight is off you and on what you want to provide. Your focus transfers from personality to values, and you're free. Ego disappears, and thoughts such as "How am I doing?" dissolve.

**4. It generates balance in your life.** One of the most common complaints I've heard from people over the years is that their lives are out of balance. Too much time and attention are being spent in one or two areas of their lives and not enough in others. The cost is high.

Too many times in the course of my work I've met middle-aged workaholics who have turned around after twenty years of Type A behavior to discover that they're alone and that it is almost impossible to rebuild the bridges that could easily have been kept in good order as the years went by—without, I believe, any cost to their business success. In fact, the result may have been quite the opposite.

Working from the perspective of roles ensures that nothing is left out of your life. One important aspect of the Best Year Yet process is a short weekly review session in which you think about your roles and what's most important to achieve in each of them for the coming week. By doing this you provide checkpoints for yourself and move step by step toward the goals you have for the next year. Momentum builds and your personal strength and power grow as you become more true to yourself and what's important to you. (The full system is outlined in the discussion of Question Ten.)

This easy method helps you to make sure you don't disappear down a dark hole with a total focus on just one role or one project within one role of your life. While I obviously spend more time in some roles than others over the course of a week, I'm doing my best to accomplish something important in each role. I'm able to make valuable distinctions between intention and time. It takes a surprisingly short amount of time to make a warm connection, for example, with someone in my family.

Much of life's stress, anxiety, and depression comes from being more narrow and limited in your life focus than you really want to be. I have embarrassing memories of several times in my past when I became so caught up with a new man that I let everything else slip. In the end I always lost both my self and the relationship.

**5. It increases your natural motivation.** When you're making what you think and feel are the right choices for you and you're seeing them through, your momentum and natural energy increase. This positive cycle becomes self-perpetuating and you're naturally pushed to make the changes you want to make—not to get better but to become more effective in playing your roles.

> ◈ **When we're being true to ourselves and doing what really matters to us, we are living our lives with integrity.**

One of the biggest lessons I have learned is that much suffering comes from a lack of integrity. When you've integrated your roles, you have the life design that can help you to live with integrity. Energy and enthusiasm return, and it's no trouble to keep going—you can't stop yourself.

# What Are Your Roles?

As you define your roles, remember that this is your list just for now. It's often necessary to drop old roles, add new ones, or change some as circumstances change.

Think first about the roles you're currently playing:

- What are my current responsibilities?

- What am I accountable for in my life?

- What do I do during the day? The weekends?

- What would I call the role I'm playing as I'm doing each of these activities?

Consider the roles you're not actively focused on now but feel you should be doing more with. For instance, are your relationships with your parents what you want them to be? Maybe you haven't given attention to the role of son or daughter over the past several years, but now want that to change. If that is the case, this role would then be on your current list of roles.

Give your imagination a chance, too. What roles are there that you are not playing but would like to play? When I wrote this book, the role of writer entered my list of roles, although when the year started and I did my Best Year Yet process, I hadn't yet written a word. Putting it on the list got me going. How about painter, adventurer, actor, student, salesperson, sailor—what dream role do you have?

Here are names others have given to the roles they play in their lives:

| | |
|---|---|
| Parent | Lover |
| Son, daughter | Husband |
| Family member | Wife |
| Homeowner | Cook |
| Manager | Deacon |
| Receptionist | Homemaker |
| Fund-raiser | Friend |
| Director | Poet |
| Salesperson | Designer |
| My own coach | Adventurer |

Above all, I believe one of your roles needs to focus on taking care of yourself—being your own coach or caretaker. However you want to name this role, and in spite of being engaged in Life Pursuit II, you must take care of yourself so you can take care of others and carry out your responsibilities. You are the one who plays these roles and needs the strength, stamina, health, and inspiration to live according to your values. As you review your performance and your intentions for each role every week, you'll be able to think about what you want or what you need to do for yourself. A life shaped around Life Pursuit II does not ignore the self—quite the opposite. It's impossible to play other roles with any degree of effectiveness if you're worn out, stressed, and resentful.

Once you've made your full list of roles, count them. How many are there on your list? If there are more than seven or eight, I strongly recommend that you consolidate several roles to narrow your focus. Just as managers must limit the number of employees they manage in order to stay sane and be able to direct, coach, and empower each person, you should limit your roles in order to win at self-management. Give up the complicated life and avoid the feeling of being overwhelmed. Set yourself up to win.

> *Our life is frittered away by detail.*
> *Simplify, Simplify!*
>
> HENRY DAVID THOREAU

This year my roles are:

1. Jinny's coach
2. Writer
3. Coach

4. Wife

5. Mother

6. Family member

7. Friend

8. Homemaker

In order to simplify, everything to do with taking care of the home, car, and money is included in my role as homemaker. My relationships with Tim's parents and our aunts, uncles, sisters, brothers, nieces, and nephews make up my role as family member.

Think about the roles you're currently playing, feel you should play more, or want to add to your life. List them, remembering to integrate roles so that you have no more than eight main roles to consider as you go forward in the Best Year Yet process.

## My current roles:

1. _____

2. _____

3. _____

4. _____

5. _____

6. _____

7. _____

8. _____

# Linking Roles and Personal Values

You now have two valuable pieces of information about yourself: your personal values and your roles. In order to begin to integrate the two into your thinking, look at the graph below:

| | PERSONAL VALUES | | | | | | | |
|---|---|---|---|---|---|---|---|---|
| | Love | Honesty | Trust | Integrity | Doing My Best | Empathy | Responsibility | Empowerment |
| Personal Coach | X | X | | | | X | X | |
| Manager | | | X | X | X | | | X |
| Salesman | | | | X | | | X | |
| Husband and Father | X | X | X | | | X | | X |
| Church Member | X | | | | X | X | X | |
| Family Member | X | | | | | | X | |
| Friend | | X | X | | | X | | |
| Homeowner | | | | | X | | X | |

**ROLES** (left side)

Importance of Values in Each Role

This man has listed his roles down the left-hand side of the graph and his personal values across the top. He can now do several important bits of thinking in order to clarify how he wishes to demonstrate his personal values in different aspects of his life. In this example he has thought through each of his roles, asking himself, "Is this value of *major* importance in this role?" Obviously there's space for each value in each role, but in order to begin to shape each specific role, he chose values that he felt were vital to his success in each role.

Here is a form for you to use for your own thinking—or you can make a simple graph of your own on a pad of paper.

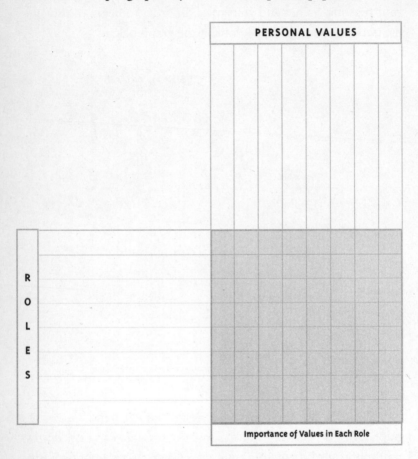

In addition to going through the process of deciding which key values you want to demonstrate in each role, you can also carry out a quick self-assessment on the same form. How do you feel your current behavior is reflected in each role? Use a different-colored pen and check the values you're currently demonstrating in specific roles. Go down the column for each value, checking the roles where you feel you're demonstrating this value in the way you want to. In doing this you find out where your journey begins, and you start with a positive focus.

You can now point yourself in an outward direction and become more proactive in the planning of your own life. A natural outcome is that you start to ask yourself such questions as:

- How am I going to help my son?

- What can I do to insure that I get the raise I need?

- When can I find some time with my husband?

- If I'm really going to write a book, what's the first step?

- What does my mother need from me?

Consciousness increases and begins to shape your life in new and more empowering ways. I've found that living with a focus on roles and personal values has reduced stress and increased my sense of fulfillment. I now have a method for making sense of things and bringing myself back into balance on a regular basis.

I know it takes courage and determination to appreciate more deeply who you are and what you want in your life, but the experience is profound and worth every ounce of discipline it takes to make yourself do it. Your personal values and your intentions for each role take the lead in your life and give it shape and direction. Be selfish for a short time now so you can decide where you stand and what you stand for.

One of the principal benefits of directing our lives in this way is an increased sense of purpose, making it easier to answer tricky questions such as "Who am I?" and "What am I doing here?" or "What's the point?"

## How Do You Intend to Play Each Role?

Although Best Year Yet is focused just on the next year of your life, you can start to envision a longer-term view of how you want to live each role. Once you can see a picture in your mind, you'll naturally be drawn to living in that way.

Take just ten minutes to look at your list of roles. Quickly focus on each role, one at a time, and see yourself acting in the role in the way that would most demonstrate what's important to you and that would match your values. As you go through each role, ask yourself, "How will it look? Feel? Sound?"

Think about how you would like to be seen carrying out each of your roles. This is just preliminary thinking and planning, but through it you start to plant the seeds that can grow into your greater effectiveness in each role. What are the outcomes you'd like as a result of playing each role? As you begin to direct yourself to live your roles with more awareness, what guidelines or advice do you have for yourself?

- In my role as a wife, I want to do more appreciating and less complaining.

- As a husband, I'd like to listen more fully to my wife.

- When I talk to my son, I want to ask more questions and really listen to what he has to say.

- I want to be more honest and helpful with my friends, letting them know what I really feel.

- With each person in my family, I want to spend more time thanking and praising than dispensing my infinite wisdom.

- At the office I want to speak up and say what I think.

As you answer Questions Seven and Eight of Best Year Yet, you'll begin to focus on your goals for the next year of your life. Having seen the bigger picture in your mind's eye helps you identify what steps you want to take and what changes you want to instigate in the next year, knowing that each moves you toward the future you're creating.

Do remember your most important role: taking care of yourself. What do you want to do for yourself to help you to be able to fulfill these roles in the way you want? What advice do you have for yourself so that, for example, you can be loving, healthy, calm, and happy as you play each role?

As you envision yourself in your roles, give major attention to succeeding in this important one, looking after yourself. It's essential to look after yourself in order to be stronger and more resilient—to be able to stand at the center of your life rather than getting buffeted around by external forces.

# Which Role Is My Major Focus for the Next Year?

*Never mention the worst. Drop it out of your consciousness.*
*This practice will bring all of your powers to focus on the*
*attainment of the best. It will bring the best to you.*

NORMAN VINCENT PEALE

## The Whole Life Review

Before deciding which role will be your main focus for the next year, give yourself some altitude in your thinking about your life and the roles you play in it. Imagine you're in a helicopter rising above your life, looking down at everything at once. See yourself scurrying around carrying out your roles and responsibilities. Allow yourself to take a neutral view of what you do and who you are—to assess the whole of your life before deciding where to focus your efforts in the next year.

The purpose of the seventh step in the Best Year Yet process is to create a breakthrough in your life by selecting one of your roles as your major focus of attention. Other roles will have goals as well, but there will be one area where you'll want or need to make the most improvement or biggest change right now.

As you look down at your life, assess how things are at present. Are some aspects of your life more satisfying and rewarding than others? Is there an overall balance in your life, or do you spot some aspects that need readjustment? What's missing in your life right now? Is something getting too much attention? Something else too little?

The following Whole Life Review model is designed to help you assess your current life and your performance in each of your current roles. It illustrates how you rate your performance in each of your roles as you begin the next year of your life. It also allows you to see clearly the degree to which you feel in balance.

Here is my Whole Life Review, done at the beginning the year I wrote this book. Notice that each spoke of the wheel represents one of my roles. I rated my performance on each of these roles on a scale of 1 to 10. It gave me the chance to think about my whole life before choosing my major focus for the year.

As I was not writing at all at the time, writer was a new role for me. I rated it at 1, my lowest score. I had been investing a great deal of time and energy into my roles as wife and coach, and the results were satisfying, so I rated my performance at 9 on both.

My rating as homemaker was 7.5—I was satisfied with the income I was making, and my car, although eight years old, was still running fine. But I was frustrated because many things that I wanted to do around the home were not getting done. There were overstuffed files, piles of photos waiting to be put into an album, meals were overfamiliar, and the plants were drooping or dead . . . I'm sure you get the picture. Certainly I was not living my values as the maker of a home and all that means to me. So, overall, a 7.5.

My area of greatest concern at this point was my performance

in taking care of myself as Jinny's coach. This was not a new reve-
lation. I was exhausted and had health problems that I was coping
with but not taking care of. While I exercised every day, I wasn't
eating well, had put on weight, and was feeling like a blob. Therefore, a 4.5. This highlighted my need to make changes here. It's
easy to see by looking at my Whole Life Review where I was out of
balance and where I needed and wanted to make improvements.

A blank Whole Life Review model has been provided. Before
you rate your performance in each of your roles, take a minute to
imagine a rating of 10 on each one (be wary of the temptation to
think you could never earn a 10 on any role). How would you be

Which Role Is My Major Focus for the Next Year?    **133**

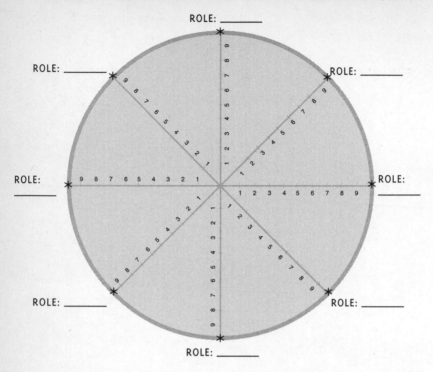

acting and behaving if you were achieving a 10 in this role? What results would you see? What would your relationship be like? You are setting your own standards here, so please yourself.

If you have fewer than eight roles, you might want to draw your own circle with the appropriate number of spokes. If you have more, consolidate and integrate your roles until you have eight.

## Using Your Whole Life Review

1. At the end of each spoke write the name of one of your life roles.

2. Notice that there are ten segments to each line. Use these to rate your performance on a scale of 1 to 10, with 10—the asterisk at the end of the line—being the highest. For example, if you're completely satisfied with your performance, rate yourself a 10; if you're 50 percent satisfied, give yourself a 5. If you're not doing anything at all or your performance is abysmal, you'll probably give yourself a 1.

3. Place a dot on each line at the point of your rating.

4. Join the dots as I did to assess your overall level of performance and to see a picture of your state of balance.

As you look at the results of your Whole Life Review, ask yourself:

• What do these results mean to me?

• What do I see in this overview of my life?

• In which role am I performing the worst? The best?

• What do I need or want to change first?

Let your intuition direct your thinking, and listen to the internal messages, both negative and positive. Do your best to make the process validating rather than invalidating. Increase your awareness of yourself as the watcher or the observer—the Chairman of the Board. Use this opportunity to make a neutral assessment of the current reality of your life.

Begin to consider which one of these roles needs your major focus over the next year of your life.

# Why Focus?

Life looks less complex and makes more sense when we're engaged in this kind of life review process. As soon as you complete your Best Year Yet workshop, however, the busyness of your life will take over again. In order to stay on the path to the changes you want to make when the day-to-day challenges of living reappear, it's vital to select one area of focus that will steer you through your next year. It may sound easy, but the unexpected interruptions and changes will come as they always do.

 **Simplify your life by increasing your ability to focus. Harness your power in one main direction to achieve the kind of change you want to make.**

Think of the Whole Life Review wheel: How do you want it to look in a year's time? Focusing your energies on one role brings an improvement in performance purely as a result of your awareness.

When you were a child, did you ever do the experiment with the magnifying glass? We were asked to find a dry leaf and let the sunlight pass through the magnifying glass to a spot on the leaf. Before long the leaf caught fire at the exact point where the sun's rays were focused. By directing the energy and power of the sun, something happened and change occurred.

Your personal focus and awareness work in the same way. If you want something to happen, focus on it. Just as the energy and power of the sun set the leaf on fire, you can create combustion in your life.

**◈ Give yourself a chance to win the game you're creating for yourself. When there is one role on which you're focused, you find new levels of persistence and determination. Your true self prevails.**

As you look at your Whole Life Review, you might ask, "Can't I have more than one focus?" If your chart looks like mine, it seems as if we must have two or more in order to get back the balance we want. However, I chose Jinny's coach as my major focus, with an emphasis on my health. Making myself feel better has, after all, a positive impact on my performance in all roles. I saw that focusing on this role would help me to add the new role of writer to my plate with a possibility of success. Notice that although writer had the lowest score on my wheel, I didn't select it as my major focus. Think carefully, and then choose the focus that will make the most difference to you.

Having two or more points of focus is a contradiction in terms. In this situation there is no longer a focus, and the results can't be the same. One woman who attended our workshops for many years always had difficulty choosing: "How can I choose between my role as a mother and my role as a shop owner? I don't want to give up either, and I need a breakthrough in both. It would be irresponsible to choose one over the other." Eventually, she always found that she had to choose one; otherwise both suffered. She realized that she could, without guilt or confusion, choose the one that was right for her at that moment in her life, and the result would affect all of her roles.

If you find yourself wanting to focus on two roles, ignore your inner pleas. There may be a feeling that you want to push hard now that you've decided to take charge of your life. But trying to do too much at once will be difficult and might lead you to give up altogether. Then you'd have a bigger problem than having only one major focus—you'd have none.

# How to Choose

To help you select your major focus, ask yourself these questions:

- If I could put one problem behind me, once and for all, what would it be?

- In which role do I want to have a breakthrough?

- If I were able to put a big check beside one of my roles at the end of the year, signifying that I felt a sense of mastery in that role, which would it be?

- What's the biggest impediment to my success and happiness right now?

- Which aspect of my life is the biggest drain on my energy and willingness to go for it in life?

When we think about it, there is often one aspect that's the principal barrier for us. Increase your awareness of the biggest ball and chain you're dragging, the one that's weighing you down so you're not able to express yourself fully.

When I thought about these questions in my own Best Year Yet review, focusing on my role as Jinny's coach and taking care of my health became the obvious choice. I began to imagine racing through my busy life without pain and exhaustion—moving lightly with great energy—and it was clear to me which role would pay me back the greatest return on the time and energy I invested.

Perhaps, as I did, you'll find your major focus by thinking about the different areas of your life rather than the roles you play. These are the role subsets such as money, career, children, health, fitness, long-range planning, love life, and marriage. Again, where do you want a breakthrough?

## Major Focus

If you do select an area of your life or a specific challenge as your major focus for this year, which role will empower you to succeed with your aim? Choose one role as your major focus—the one that will provide a gateway for the result you want. This role is your major focus.

In addition to taking much better care of my health, I've already improved my overall performance as my own coach. I find myself listening more to my own good advice and breaking the habit of putting myself at the end of my own "to do" list. Having a role as your major focus reminds you to center yourself in your role and your values as you go for your breakthrough.

Once you've chosen your major focus, write it down. Then take a bit of time to visualize the success you want to create in this role. What specific and measurable differences do you want to see? What are your criteria for success? What intangible experiences and feelings do you want as a result of achieving this change?

Start to paint a scene in your mind. What would change? What would improve? What would bring a big smile to your face?

Think about what you want others to notice and say. Consider the benefits that you want them to experience as a result of your new expertise in living this role. Create a clear mental picture of exactly what you want.

Before you move on from thinking about your major focus, dare to say what you want—and beware of your limiting paradigms. If they cloud your view, remember your new empowering paradigm. Write it down on a piece of paper, and below it write your major focus. See yourself making a quantum leap in your effectiveness in this role, empowered by this paradigm.

 **Remember that what you focus on is what you get—focusing your awareness on this role will generate the result you want.**

# It Pays to Focus

You've now chosen one area of your garden to get special attention this year. As a result, your entire garden can be much happier and healthier. Focusing on one area may raise the standard of the whole.

One of my first clients was starting his own business and found himself in the driver's seat for the first time in his career. His investors were pushing him hard to capture major accounts in order to establish the business with a strong base. But he'd never sold a thing in his life and, at this early stage, he couldn't afford to hire a salesperson. So his major focus for the year was salesperson—and he hated it!

He recounted stories of forcing himself to pick up the phone and make fifteen contacts a day. He had to push his hand toward the receiver every time, and he'd never been so uncomfortable. But he did it, and his focus paid off. By the end of the year he had a couple of major accounts, and overall sales had increased by a factor of ten.

Another older client also focused on his role as salesperson because he wanted to achieve his dream of being one of the top twenty salespeople at the major insurance company he worked for. Every year he struggled and tried, but he never made it to the top. He started by creating a paradigm of success and then visualized his name moving up the list—in his mind he actually saw his name move up the list of the top players.

As a result, he began to do all the smart things at once. He realized it was not a lack of knowing what to do that was holding him back. It was a lack of doing it. Success built on success, and when the results were announced at the end of the year, his name was right where he wanted it—on the list of top salespeople.

Another client had a more intangible major focus. The role was personal development and the specific goal was "Crack limiting personal belief systems once and for all!" He attacked the goal with great determination and was able to put his old internal conversation behind him. As a result of his persistence, he was able to stop procrastinating and start taking a stronger leadership role in his company, focusing on his strengths and achievements rather than worrying about other people's opinions of him.

Remember: your major focus is not the only thing you'll do this year, just the most important to you.

# What Are My Goals for Each Role?

*'Tis not what man does which exalts him,*
*But what man would do!*

ROBERT BROWNING

## The Power of Goals

People who have goals achieve more results in their lives.

No matter how you define success, achievement is greater among those who have clearly defined goals. It's merely common sense that people who know where they're going have a better chance of getting there. If you don't know your destination you risk going around in circles, living a life in which you exist but don't really grow and progress.

In my experience the goal factor is the most important distinguishing characteristic of truly effective people. It is far more important, for example, than a person's education or intelligence. Even those who want to meditate on a mountaintop have clearly defined goals.

A goal is a specific and measurable result you want to achieve within a specific time frame. It directs you to a destination, a result, a salary, a career, a relationship—something that you haven't yet acquired or experienced in your life.

The results of a study of business school graduates who had been out of school for at least ten years illustrates the power of goals. Upon graduation, 83 percent had no goals, while 14 percent had vague goals in their minds but no written goals. Only 3 percent had clearly articulated, written goals. When their level of accomplishment was compared ten years later, those with *some* sense of their goals earned three times more than the ones with no goals, and the 3 percent with written goals earned ten times more than those with none at all!

But goals alone are not nearly enough. The setting and achieving of goals may bring a certain brand of success in one narrow aspect of life such as material reward or career promotion, but this does not generate an overall sense of fulfillment. Remember the fallen gods of the 1980s? How many people on their deathbeds wish they'd spent more time at the office?

**People whose goals are aligned with their values achieve more satisfaction and fulfillment. When we've achieved a goal that has been driven by our values, by what we believe in and what's really important to us, we experience a flow to our lives and a sense of fulfillment in our hearts and minds.**

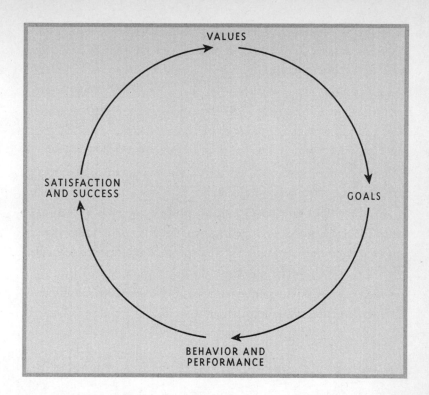

VALUES

GOALS

BEHAVIOR AND
PERFORMANCE

SATISFACTION
AND SUCCESS

Value-driven goals lead to behavior and performance that express who we are. This in turn leads to the success and satisfaction that we've been longing for. The more we repeat this cycle, the more it reinforces our values and our commitment to live in a way that creates a self-perpetuating and self-affirming cycle.

Living within the framework of value-driven goals gives a positive shape to the way you think and feel about your life. You focus on what you want rather than what you don't want, thus providing specific direction and focus for your life. You can move from complaint to action and gain a new degree of momentum, actually moving toward your dreams. A switch takes place and you feel a lift. I can see the sanity return for clients when I say to them, "I understand from what you're saying that you know what you *don't* want. Now, can you tell me what you *do* want?"

When you set goals and write them down, you've expressed your willingness to be responsible for living with integrity—doing what you know to do in order to be true to yourself and your values. Goals pull your talent from you and force you to come up with the goods—not only achieving your goal, but discovering and using more of your potential.

Starting with the end in mind pulls both your action and your attitude toward your goals. Your talents, your intelligence, and your awareness are pointed at a specific target, and your consolidation of energies brings results in a way the scattered approach fails to do. You know whether you're going to Boston, Boulder, or Bologna, and you're on your way.

**Goals guide you to be responsible and proactive in your life. The more specific and measurable your goals, the more willing you are to be responsible for making them happen.**

# Powerful Goals

When you change from wishing and whining to setting powerful value-driven goals, you move toward a more positive and productive life. Negative emotions like frustration, fear, anxiety, stress, anger, and depression plague people with no direction and therefore no focus or hope. Setting goals moves us from dreams with a remote possibility and reliance on blind luck to the results and relationships we're looking for. Living life with the attitude "Let's wait and see how it turns out" is a waste of your potential and your power.

Powerful goals are specific. They are defined in words that give you a clear and concise mental image of what you want to achieve. You know from reading the goal exactly what you want. The more specific your goal, the more quickly you'll see what to do and be able to find the resources to achieve it.

| | |
|---|---|
| **Nonspecific goal:** | Spend more time with my children. |
| **Specific goal:** | Read to my children for at least thirty minutes three times a week. |
| | |
| **Nonspecific goal:** | Improve my performance at work. |
| **Specific goal:** | Find out exactly what I need to do to get a promotion and a 5 percent pay raise, and do it. |
| | |
| **Nonspecific goal:** | Reduce my stress level and increase my peace of mind. |
| **Specific goal:** | Meditate at least fifteen minutes each morning. |

Powerful goals must also be measurable. How many? How big? How often? You quantify each goal so that you'll be in no doubt at the end of the year whether you've won or lost the game or how close you came. If you want a raise, how much? So many wealthy people are still working as hard now that they're fifty-year-old millionaires as they were when they were twenty-five-year-old hopefuls, and they are paying a big price as a result. They've never slowed down to reap the rewards of their success. They don't understand how to cut back since they're unsure whether their goal of becoming rich has been achieved. They never answered the question "How much is enough?" I've seen many, many examples of this.

Powerful goals must also be set in a time frame. Since you're setting goals for the next year of your life, your commitment exists within a definite amount of time. Limiting the time available to achieve your goal establishes focus. Goals without a deadline are as meaningless as a football game without an agreed ending time.

But once you've set your annual goals, you may want to set deadlines for milestones throughout the year. For example:

| | |
|---|---|
| **Annual goal:** | Do a form of aerobic exercise four times a week and lose fifteen pounds. |
| **Three-month milestone:** | Jog three times a week and lose four pounds. |
| **Annual goal:** | Write my first book and find an agent and publisher. |
| **Three-month milestone:** | Write chapter outline and contact three potential agents. |

Commitment to a deadline for achieving a goal adds momentum and certainty. You're on your way, and this is a great antidote to procrastination. And the earlier you get started, the more time you have to achieve your goal, and therefore the better your chance of success.

Powerful goals start with strong, active verbs. They mark the start of your goal, which will be a simple and complete sentence stating clearly the result you want. Verbs clarify what needs to be done, stimulate a call to action, and clearly describe exactly what you want to do. For example:

- Give
- Earn
- Join
- Practice
- Write
- Spend time
- Complete
- Arrange
- Plan
- Get
- Choose
- Invest
- Achieve
- Learn
- Work
- Ensure
- Make
- Meet

Starting your goals with these kinds of words gives you direction and gets the momentum going the minute you write them down.

Finally, learn the distinction between result goals and process goals—best distinguished by the following examples:

| | |
|---|---|
| **Result goal:** | Achieve sales target of $250,000. |
| **Process goal:** | Make twenty new sales calls each week. |
| **Result goal:** | Lose twenty pounds. |
| **Process goal:** | Eat 1200 calories a day with 20 percent or fewer calories from fat. |
| **Result goal:** | Improve communication and connection with my sons. |
| **Process goal:** | Write to my sons every week. |

Take time to consider which type of goal is more likely to ensure that your behavior will be appropriate to achieve the result you actually want. For instance, for years I had weight-loss goals—a result goal. Once I switched to a process goal that I knew would guarantee the result, I attained the goal. Process goals define the action we think will lead us to our goal. And, as the point is to make life sweeter on the way to our goals, process goals provide a strong incentive to continue, with rewards along the way. (Remember to celebrate your achievements and congratulate yourself every time you achieve a process goal!)

However, some goals are far more powerful if they are expressed as result goals. It often takes more courage for me to set this kind of goal, specifically in the areas of business, money, and fund-raising. Once I learned to make this level of commitment and deliver, however, I was able to take on bigger and bigger challenges and make them happen. Sticking my neck out in this way forced me to dig into myself and come up with the ability to achieve the goal—and, I believe, doing so has pulled out far more of my potential than if I hadn't made such big promises.

**Powerful goals are simple, clear instructions for you and your awareness. You now know where the bull's-eye is located and have an excellent chance of hitting it.**

# Goal Setting

It's time to begin to write your goals for your best year yet.

As you switch to Life Pursuit II, you start by setting goals shaped by your personal values. This step alone brings you closer to a life of integrity and satisfaction. While these goals will address your basic wants and needs, they will also—more importantly—lead you to a life in which you're true to yourself and therefore fulfilled.

If you have identified your lifetime goals and have a personal vision or mission, some of your annual goals become self-evident as the next step on the way to achieving your longer-term goals. As much as possible, set your goals in the context of your bigger plan.

Tim and I have been working for years on our Best Decade Yet plan, which is designed to enable us to take a sabbatical year and really enjoy ourselves. This has focused many of our short-term goals and made it much easier for us to make choices that further this dream. As soon as we first made this plan, we changed our spending habits. We cut back on the money we used for eating out, vacations, and clothes, and increased our mortgage payments. Each year we set goals for savings, reduced the mortgage and other debts, and learned more about the places we want to visit and adventures we hope to have in that year.

## SETTING GOALS IN THE CONTEXT OF A LIFE PLAN

Use whatever level of awareness you currently have about your long-term goals. Perhaps this exercise will stimulate you to apply the technology of Best Year Yet to the planning of your life.

As you begin setting your goals, make sure you've thought through which areas of your life are related to each of your roles.

For example, the role of self-manager or personal coach typically includes such areas as health, fitness, education, skill-building, relaxation, and fun. In the worksheet we use for this step, there is a space for noting related areas and aspects of each role.

The man whose goals are listed below includes his children, their school fees, and their presents as areas to consider in his role of father. See how he thought through the different aspects of his role, and notice how doing this helped him to define his goals for this role.

To set your goals, begin by selecting one of your roles and writing down all the related areas of your life. Then jot down the goals you have for yourself for the next year, remembering the guidelines for setting powerful goals. Follow your intuition and listen to your inner voice. Rather than this being a difficult part of

---

**ROLE:** Father
_____

Areas included: __Joe_____  __Julia_____  Presents____

__Mark_____  __School fees_____  _____

GOALS:
- Plan a special weekend once a month with each child.
- Make sure Julia understands her math.
- Pick out a special present for each in early December.
- Express praise and appreciation more than correction.
_____
_____
_____
_____

---

What Are My Goals for Each Role?   153

the process, most people find it easy to concentrate as they begin to give specific shape to their next year.

For most of us, at this point there's a mental rubbing of hands. Finally, some sanity! You've worked through the first seven steps of the process and you've cleared your mind and made some space for yourself. Your natural enthusiasm is uncovered again, and it's time to plant your garden in the rich soil you've prepared.

Remember to set a clear goal for your major focus. In Part Three you'll find more forms like the one above for setting goals for each of your roles.

# One Final Check

One last step before finalizing your goals for your best year yet: a final pass to ensure that you have the best possible chance of achieving your goals. The purpose of this step is to ensure that you are committed to each of your goals, that each has a reasonable chance of success.

Go through your list of goals, thinking carefully about each and asking yourself such questions as:

- Will I make sure this happens?

- Am I merely hoping this will be achieved simply because it's on the list?

- Am I *going* to do this?

- Is this goal specific and measurable? Does it start with a verb?

- Is it a result or a process goal? Have I made the right choice?

Make sure that your goals:

- match your values;

- are not "should" goals;

- are ones you want badly enough to do what it takes; and

- are ones you're willing to be responsible for.

# Match Your Personal Values to Your Goals

Above all, make sure that the goal is aligned with your values. Place your list of personal values beside you as you review your goals. Catch goals that could lead you away from your values. For example, a goal to earn more money might lead you to work longer hours and jeopardize your goal to spend more time with your children. Is it worth it? Is it necessary to work longer hours in order to earn more? Be wary of goals whose means don't justify the end result.

Remember the cost of goals that are not aligned with your values. Can you afford even one year in which you waste energy and intelligence pursuing a goal that violates one of your personal values? If you're in doubt, perhaps the goal is one that chases Life Pursuit I—proving yourself. If so, give it a toss!

# Avoid "Should" Goals

Many teachers have reminded me not to "should" on myself!

Are any of your goals ones you feel you should do but don't really want to do? First ask yourself if your goal is aligned with your principles. If it is and you can see that it's something you really would like to do, shift your attitude to the goal from *should* to *want* or *will*. If you can't do this, cross it off your list.

Sometimes our *should*s are tired old goals. Let them go. Often we've had goals for decades and never consciously stopped wanting them. When you were seven years old, you wanted a fancy bicycle but you never received it. Now that you've grown, it's time to let go of the "bicycles" in your life.

For example, do you have a dream weight or size that you haven't seen since you were seventeen? Let it go. Get to a healthy weight and size and drop the impossible fantasy. For years I tried to get to 120 pounds. Every bite I put into my mouth and every shopping trip was in the context of *Not 120 pounds!* What a relief it was to finally give up that unrealistic goal.

What are the "bicycles" in your life? Give yourself a break and get them off your list.

# Connect to Your Real Wants

The question of whether I really *wanted* to do something was a confusing issue for me until I made a distinction between little wants and big wants.

Little wants are really don't wants. The lazy me never wants to crawl out from under the covers. I want to stay in bed! I mean, who really wants to leap out of bed in the morning? And for sure I wanted to keep smoking, not to give it up. Give me the easy life. It's so easy to follow this kind of want—sure I'd rather watch television than write letters or pay bills. I much prefer the extra half hour of sleep to going out in the cold to exercise.

 **Endless procrastination, disappointment, and lack of self-respect are the products of the little wants.**

But these little wants are not what I *really* want. Big wants are characterized by their connection to my personal values, and they further my commitment to Life Pursuit II. The achievement of goals in this category is worth the discipline needed for me to make sure they happen. Without this type of goal, I'd rarely grow or make the contribution I'd like to make.

The big wants have more integrity than the little wants and give you the environment in which you can express yourself.

# Responsibility

If you're not willing to do whatever you need to do to achieve the goal, you're probably not going to be responsible for achieving that goal. For each of your goals, you must be motivated to give it your best shot. Otherwise, scratch it.

In order to achieve these goals, you'll need to focus on them throughout the year. There are probably plenty of goals on your list—get rid of the ones you're not going to take responsibility for.

# What Are My Top Ten Goals
# for the Next Year?

*People are always blaming their circumstances for
what they are. The people who get on in this world are the
people who look for the circumstances they want, and,
if they can't find them, make them.*

GEORGE BERNARD SHAW

## Why Limit Myself to Ten?

When we first started to set goals for the year ahead, Tim and I
each had over one hundred goals written on our stack of three-by-
five index cards. We had one card for each role, and most had
goals written on both sides of the card. A few roles even had several cards stapled together. We failed to limit ourselves by selecting the ones that were most important to us. The goals sat on the
list together, each having the same amount of weight, attention,
and focus. There were simply too many.

While we each did well simply because we'd taken the time to
identify roles and set goals for each of them, we robbed ourselves

of the satisfaction of creating a game we could win. In doing so we decreased our overall effectiveness and it became too easy to let our attention drift away from our intentions for the year. I gave up on many of my goals early in the year because I just didn't have the time for them. I'd set myself an impossible task, but still felt guilty because I couldn't fulfill it. A mistake and a lesson.

While I'm not suggesting that you need to *eliminate* all but ten of the goals you've set, I strongly recommend that you select the ten that are most important to you. You can certainly work on the rest of your goals and achieve them. But selecting your top ten allows you to focus your power in a laserlike way and therefore increase the amount of intelligence and consciousness you can commit to each one. A list of your top ten goals for the next year gives you a map with which to plan your journey. You'll find it easier to attract the support and resources necessary to get to your destination.

When I look at my list of top ten goals and I know I'm satisfied with the goals I've selected, I get that feeling of *"Can do!"* I can't wait to get started, and I have a strong belief in myself and my ability to stick to the plan and make it happen. It looks possible.

**The quality of thinking you need to do in order to select your most important goals forces you to make the choices that will guarantee balance in your life and the experience of being true to yourself—the feeling that you're going to make true progress in the coming year of your life.**

# How to Choose

Start by reviewing your responses to the first seven questions. Remember what you've learned about yourself and what's most important to you. Think about the lessons you've learned and the guidelines you've established for your next year. Remind yourself of your new paradigm and your personal values.

To start the process of selection, turn back to your Whole Life Review and the thinking that led you to choose your major focus. What's going to make the most difference to you in this next year? As you answer these questions and carry out this review, begin to consider prioritizing your goals and choosing the ones that matter most.

## MY TOP TEN GOALS FOR NEXT YEAR

1. _____
2. _____
3. _____
4. _____
5. _____
6. _____
7. _____
8. _____
9. _____
10. _____

As you've been taking yourself through the Best Year Yet process, what vision have you started to create for your next year? Think about what you really want for yourself and for those people who are most important to you. Consider the benefits inherent in achieving your most important goals—both for yourself and for others. Which goals, when achieved, will make the most difference to you and them?

Once you've completed this preliminary thinking, return to the list of goals you set for each of your roles. First highlight or circle the ones that are "musts" for your list of ten. The obvious ones. Then add up the number you've selected and figure out how many more you can select to make up your list of ten.

Write down your first-draft list of ten so you can look at them together. Visualize yourself in a year's time having achieved each of these goals. How will you feel then? Will you be thrilled with what you've achieved? Do the goals motivate you to keep going until they're reached? Make sure that you're genuinely enthusiastic about the end you have in mind. Don't sell out. Is it enough, at least for now? If not, find out what's missing and add it.

Next, consider whether meeting these ten goals is possible. Can you do it? Look through your list to catch conflicting goals and ask yourself if there's a way you can achieve both goals without sacrificing your values or, perhaps, your health. Dig up any lingering thoughts and doubts and address them. How can you overcome them? Either see how to make it work or switch some of the goals for others you didn't select at first.

Check your list to make sure that each role has at least one goal, so that your plan leads you to a more balanced life and lifestyle. As you imagine yourself walking and running through the next year of your life, make sure you're happy with the balance of work and play. I recommend that at least one goal on your list be for pure fun or pleasure—at least one you're *really* looking forward to having or doing. This is your life, right?

Finally, make sure that your top ten goals are the design for your best year yet. When you've achieved these goals, will you have had the best year you've ever had? And don't forget, whatever didn't make the cut this year can go on your list next year. The coming year is just your best year so far—they can get better and better as the years go by. Ours truly have.

# Starting to Plan Your Best Year Yet

Once you're sure that you have the right ten, look at the words and the way each goal is written. Revise, rewrite, and reword until you're completely satisfied. Keep at it until you believe that each goal is expressed perfectly and describes accurately the outcome you want.

Write each goal on a separate piece of paper or a card and place them in front of you. Look at these goals together in the context of their being the seeds you're planting in the rich soil of your intelligence and your consciousness. You now have the beginning of a plan for your best year yet. There are a few more steps to prepare your plan and make it even more powerful.

The first step is to repeat your new empowering paradigm for the year as you look at each of your goals. Notice how each different goal is empowered by this way of thinking and feeling about yourself.

The second step is to prioritize your list of goals. My favorite definition of *priority* is that which brings me the greatest return on the investment of my time and energy.

Which goal will head up your list? Using the definition above, which one is your top priority for the year? For most people it's the goal related to their major focus, so it grabs their attention every time they look at the list. Whichever it is, pick it up, turn it over, and place it to one side, knowing it will be at the top of the list.

Then look at the remaining nine goals and again ask yourself, "Of the goals left, which one will bring me the greatest return on the investment of my time and energy?"

Let your intuition guide your selection of the goal that will be second on your list. When you've selected it, turn it over and place it on top of the first goal. Repeat this process with all of your other goals until you have a prioritized list of your top ten goals.

The last step is to make a one-page summary of the four principal parts of your Best Year Yet plan:

1. Guidelines for the Year (Question Three)

2. New Paradigm (Question Four)

3. Major Focus (Question Seven)

4. Top Ten Goals (Question Nine)

Do something to make the page special. Perhaps you want to have it typed or just neatly handwritten on a piece of quality paper. Use your imagination to create this important blueprint for your best year yet—it's a special document.

Now at last you have a one-page summary of your basic plan for the next twelve months. All the work you've done to get to this point has been most important: You've clarified your intention and you know what you want. Even if you simply put your one-page summary in a drawer and didn't look at it until the end of the year, you would still have a good chance of having your best year yet. Don't underestimate the importance of the thinking you've done in answering the first nine questions.

Here is an example of one man's Best Year Yet plan. You haven't met him, but notice how much you know about him and what's important to him from looking at his plan.

### GUIDELINES
- Be cheery all the time.
- Do first things first!
- Identify and say what I want.

### NEW PARADIGM
*I'm a master at creating my own destiny.*

### MAJOR FOCUS
Company leader

### TOP TEN GOALS
1. Practice Gold Time Management every week.
2. Meditate daily.
3. Achieve our profit target for the year.
4. Make a complete plan for my retirement.
5. Do all I can to support Sue in her new career.
6. Have a special event each month for the kids.
7. Exercise five times a week and lose fifteen pounds.
8. Host a great reunion for our family.
9. Make contact with old friends.
10. Ensure all staff receive a monthly coaching session.

Look at your own page, imagining that it's not yours but someone else's. I find this shift in perspective sometimes helps me to appreciate what I've accomplished just by making my plan.

**Your one-page plan is your guide for the next year. It provides a foundation for your thinking and planning and gives you your own best advice about how to behave and perform in order to turn your plan into reality.**

This plan will form the basis of how you organize and manage yourself to achieve your goals. It helps me to make choices throughout the year and enables me to do a good job of coaching myself on a monthly and weekly basis.

Read again your own words of wisdom:

- The good advice you've given yourself with your *guidelines*

- The empowering *paradigm* to guide your perception of yourself

- Your *major focus* and the breakthrough you're going for

- Your carefully crafted list of *top ten goals* for the year

Take a minute to appreciate yourself and the clarity, direction, and sense of purpose you've created for yourself. You've now put yourself among that special group who have clearly articulated goals and a plan for their lives. However, you've gone even further. All too often those people who do set goals do so without preparing the personal environment for those goals to succeed. By answering the questions of the Best Year Yet process, you have taken the necessary steps to prepare this environment for yourself.

# How Can I Make Sure I Achieve My Top Ten Goals?

*The problem in my life and other people's lives is not the absence*
*of knowing what to do, but the absence of doing it.*

PETER DRUCKER

## Doing What You Know to Do

Ain't it the truth! The quote above summarizes one of the greatest challenges of being human. When I've taken the time to look back at some of my failures, the big ones and the little ones, I can usually see exactly what I could have done differently to improve my results.

The final question of the Best Year Yet process is designed to remind you of what you know to do, and this chapter is devoted to hints and ideas to help you do just that.

One simple key to achieving our top ten goals for the year is visibility. Keep your Best Year Yet plan in sight. Decide where to put it so you'll see it every day. You may want to put it on the wall near your desk, inside a cupboard you use frequently, or in a prominent place in your organizer. You'll need to decide how public you want to be with your goals—whatever you decide, try to find the solution that ensures *you* will see them regularly.

Again, awareness is everything. Taking just ten seconds a day to read your plan is one of the best recommendations I can make. Let it grab your attention, stimulate you to action, and refocus your intention for the year.

Now that you've made a plan for the year, the following model is invaluable in managing yourself to achieve success. It's a simple reminder of the fundamentals of the Best Year Yet process. The three angles of the triangle point to the key aspects to keep in place to make things happen. I call it E-S-P, the foolproof solution. It's not always easy, but it's a simple reminder of the basics.

E   When we're aware of the *external* factors, or what we need to *do* in order to move toward our goal, we're on our way. Take full responsibility for each goal: identify the action you need to take, and just do it.

S   Using a coach, a colleague, or a friend—any form of *support*—helps us identify what we need to do (E) and supports us to shift to our empowering paradigm (P).

P   Our *paradigm,* or the way we see the problem, can lead us to either success or failure. Removing internal obstacles makes the greatest difference to our success. Make sure that your focus on your new paradigm is receiving as much attention as your goals. Invest the time to make sure this happens.

Think of the E-S-P model as a three-legged stool. Make sure each leg is in place and working and you'll have a simple and stable platform on which to deliver your plan. Do what you need to

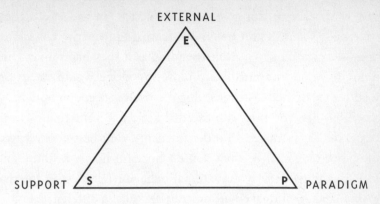

do (E), shift your paradigm to the perception that empowers you (P), and find someone to support you (S) to do the first two.

The balance between (E) and (P) is critical. I've known so many people who seem to be taking all the right action, doing what they know to do, but still their dreams elude them. The problem is usually found on the inside, shaped by a limiting paradigm that is arguing against their success the whole time they're busily working toward their goals. Ever met a beautiful person who looks and acts like the kind of person who would be pursued by many potential partners, yet is alone? Most often this is not a matter of choice, but a matter of limiting internal messages.

> ◈ **There must be a balance between the goal we want and the way we perceive our chances of success.**

Nor does it work to have a brilliant empowering paradigm and sit waiting for miracles to occur. Sometimes this happens, but taking action that furthers the result on which we've focused our positive paradigm is a guarantee of success. In the 1970s there were many courses and books advocating "prosperity consciousness." I saw too many people spending as if they had money they didn't have and hoping this philosophy alone would bring the wealth they desired. Most just dug themselves deeper into debt.

But when you put both external action and internal focus in place, the earth moves. In order to ensure your best year yet, you must not only change what you do but also how you think and feel. Changing *either* your external behavior (E) *or* your internal mental and emotional environment (P) makes a difference, but it's not enough. Positive lasting improvement comes from changing both at once. The Best Year Yet process makes sure you do this.

When we're trying to put all this together in the middle of a busy life, it's sometimes difficult to remember these simple truths. The answer lies in the third leg of the stool—support. A few people have mastered the art of self-coaching, but most of us do better if there's a friend or family member whom we meet on a regular basis to check our progress and see how we're doing. They keep us honest.

Even though we want to move into new territory, we can be so uncomfortable about it that we avoid doing what we know to do. Promising someone else that you're going to take action toward your goals or meditate on your paradigm can make all the difference. Years ago when I first wanted to start running I would promise myself day after day that I'd wake up early and get out there—but I rarely made it out the door. What finally made the difference was agreeing to meet a friend on the corner at 6:30 A.M. three mornings a week.

If you're wondering where to find someone to support you this year, consider someone else who has completed the Best Year Yet process. You can support one another. Or sometimes couples sit down once a month, review their achievements against their past month's goals, and set goals for the next month. You might ask a work colleague—a boss, subordinate, or peer—anyone who'd like to be in the kind of relationship in which the partners are committed to each other's success.

🔲 **Seek out a like-minded person in your life and provide support for one another. The secret lies in your willingness to be supported to do what you know to do.**

Use the E-S-P solution to get yourself moving again anytime you feel stuck. It's an awareness tool and a catalyst for action. Think about a particular problem or goal and answer these questions to get yourself moving again:

E    What's the next step?

S    Who can provide the support I need?

P    Does the way I see the problem lead to success?

# Pitfalls

There will be disappointments on the way, but it's possible to avoid many of them by becoming aware of some of the pitfalls and the damage they can do to your enthusiasm. Once you know about them, you can see them coming and sidestep them rather than falling into them.

Some of the most discouraging influences are the negative and disempowering messages we give ourselves. This kind of internal mental conversation is part of being human. When I hear people talk about some of their fears and doubts—some of the things they hear themselves saying to themselves—I think we must all be tuned in to the same station. They sound just like me. It's all part of the social and emotional conditioning that we've received from our environment.

The trick is to catch yourself when you're listening to this station as if it were God's truth. It's not, so change to another station—your new empowering paradigm. The station that dispenses the truth. It's hard to imagine that you'll get the internal voice to shut up. But you can control the attention you give the voice and, above all, where you focus your awareness. One lesson I've heard many times is "We're not responsible for the thoughts that come into our minds, only for what we do with them."

Another powerful pitfall is the negativity of others. I've seen people so positive and enthusiastic I thought nothing could stop them, yet one discouraging or disparaging remark from someone else dissolved their confidence. While we can't stop people who seem to want us to feel small and stupid, we can ignore them or, better still, stay away from them. Seek out people who support you and want you to succeed. Listen to motivational tapes to remind you who you are and what you can do. Read books that inspire you to do what you really want to do. Do whatever you can to build up the muscle of your heart and your awareness—your center, who you are.

Finally, beware of end-goal thinking. It goes something like this: *I don't care what I have to go through this year. I'll make any sacrifice to get what I want!* This approach doesn't lead to your best year yet. Willing yourself to succeed while gritting your teeth is not the name of the game.

⬛ **Choose your mountain not for its summit, but**

**for the climb. Enjoy the adventure!**

> *Things won are done; the joy lies in the doing.*
>
> WILLIAM SHAKESPEARE

# Gold Time

How many times have you been told that what you need to do is manage your time? Good advice, you think, but actually it's impossible. Time is unmanageable. No matter what you do or how well-organized you get, the hands of the clock go round and round. What you *can* do, however, is learn to manage yourself.

One of the greatest secrets of successful self-management is described by a simple and powerful system I call Gold Time Management. It leads us to manage ourselves by identifying the activities in each of our roles that will make the greatest difference to us and to others. The following Gold Time Management model shows how it works.

Gold Time is time spent on important, not urgent activities— activities in the upper right-hand corner of the matrix on the following page. It's called Gold Time because the time you spend on this type of activity pays off at least tenfold over the time you invest in other types of activities.

## GOLD TIME MANAGEMENT

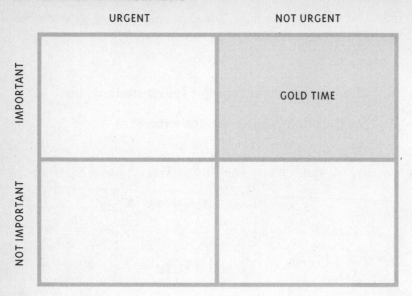

Also, as the natural progression is for things to move from being not urgent to being urgent, by focusing on activities in the upper right-hand corner you're led to a life of less stress and less fire-fighting. Fewer things reach the crisis stage. For example, as a thirty-year-old you might feel that it is very important to exercise and get fit, but it's not really urgent—it can wait.

Yes, it's so easy to wait. You're going to start sometime, but right now you're too busy. We tell ourselves, "As soon as I _____" (fill in the blank with your reason for postponing what really matters to you). Whatever it is, it comes before devoting more time to becoming fit. As the years go by and the medical checkups provide more startling feedback, the need might become more urgent. But without awareness of Gold Time, life gets eaten up by the empty promise of "As soon as I _____."

Activities that are "important, not urgent" are activities or projects that matter most to you. For example, your top ten goals for this year. Although you really do want to achieve them and know that you'll feel a lot happier and more fulfilled when you do, your resolve can be eaten up by activities in the other three segments of the model. There's too much that *must* be done (important and urgent) before you can devote time to your Best Year Yet plan.

 **But as Goethe said, "Things which matter most**

**must never be at the mercy of things which**

**matter least."**

The more responsibility you have in your life, the more essential it is to spend time in the upper right-hand corner. For example, business leaders who do not remember this spend much of their time in crisis mode and are never capable of making lasting positive change in the culture or the performance of the business.

They realize that it's vital to walk around and get to know the people in the business and listen to them, but their schedules are too full of meetings right now. They know that in order to make any sense of things they must take time out to plan for the future, but first they must prepare the speech for the industry conference next week. They know they should invest in building better relationships with their colleagues on the board, but right now they have to sort out an emergency. And so life goes on.

The process of changing to this new type of self-management is simple. Do Gold Time activities first! It makes all the difference. Doing this naturally guides us to be true to ourselves and our personal values. This focus creates integrity in the way we lead our lives. Having become better and better at this approach over the years, I have become more sane and have a greater sense of balance. I've come to realize that the only thing I can have power over is myself; when I practice Gold Time self-management, I do.

Put your top ten goals first. Put yourself and what you value first. The rest will get done. I promise. Once I've taken a step that brings me closer to one of my top ten goals or helps me to do a better job in one of my life roles, I experience such self-respect and energy that I can attack the urgent activities and get them done in far less time.

My experience has shown that the benefits of Gold Time are:

- Feelings of self-respect, being true to myself.

- Reduction in stress and anxiety.

- Improved performance in all my life roles.

- Fewer last-minute panics.

- Sense of personal power.

- Personal fulfillment.

- End of sacrifice—I'm doing far more of what really matters to me.

## The System

Setting up the system to allow you to focus on and achieve your top ten goals is not difficult. It just takes discipline and a focus on what matters most to you. The system is based on common sense, and you could easily figure it out for yourself—if you want to achieve an annual goal, take little steps regularly throughout the year and you'll get there.

Set monthly goals that represent thirty-day chunks of what needs to be done to achieve your top ten goals. Then set weekly Gold Time goals that are seven-day plans to move toward your monthly goals.

At the end of each month sit down for thirty minutes and take a good look at your Best Year Yet plan. Look at each of your top ten goals and identify the step that needs to be taken over the next month to keep you on the path toward this goal. Then, remembering the guidelines for powerful goals, set a goal that will move you closer to your best year yet. When you've achieved it, you'll see visible progress in your life.

| TOP TEN GOALS | JUNE GOALS |
|---|---|
| 1. Practice Gold Time Management. | 1. Practice Gold Time Management. |
| 2. Prepare fully for trip to India for next year. | 2. Make budget for India trip and start savings plan. |
| 3. Take better care of my mother. | 3. Phone Mother every week. |
| 4. Make annual sales target. | 4. Bring in $4000 in new business. |

5. Get fit and healthy, reducing body fat to 20 percent or less.

6. Make a list of ten books I've been meaning to read and read them.

7. See friends at least two nights a week.

8. Start a journal and keep up with it.

9. Redecorate my living room.

10. Begin a happy relationship with a woman.

5. Join a gym and work out three times a week.

6. Read *The Celestine Prophecy.*

7. Have dinner with Sam and Anita.

8. Buy the journal and write in it at least twice a week.

9. Find the gas log fire I want and buy it.

10. Phone Diane and invite her to dinner and a movie.

11. Abstain from alcohol three nights a week.

12. Phone my brother and sister.

I've found that my monthly list works best if I have no more than ten to fifteen goals. This number allows me to take a step toward each of my top ten goals and still be able to include other goals that are currently important to me in living my life roles. Then at the end of the month I review what has happened and figure out what percentage of my goals I've achieved. I rarely make 100 percent, but that doesn't matter. What matters is that I'm aware of how I'm doing and what I need to do next.

At the heart of this system is the weekly Gold Time planning session. One week is a time frame that allows us to manage ourselves to do what's most important to us and be true to ourselves. Once you get this system in place, this session takes only fifteen minutes a week.

Once a week—most people select late Friday afternoon, Sunday evening, or early Monday morning—sit down with your monthly goals and identify steps to take over the next week to further these goals. Some weeks there might be nothing to do. That's fine, but at least you've stopped to think about it.

Just as important, use this time to consider your roles. In your mind, stand in each role, one at a time, and ask yourself, "What's the most important thing I want to accomplish in this role this week? What can I do that will make the most difference in this role?" Doing this exercise naturally puts us in touch with our personal values and priorities. Then, for each of your roles, identify one specific weekly goal based on your answers to these questions.

Your list of weekly Gold Time goals is a combination of your key goals for each role and the steps needed to achieve your monthly goals.

**The weekly Gold Time planning session is not driven by your schedule nor by urgent tasks. You can still make daily "to do" lists to accomplish those kinds of things. But manage yourself to achieve your weekly Gold Time goals above all.**

## AGENDA FOR WEEKLY GOLD TIME
## PLANNING SESSION

1. Review Gold Time goals for last week and appreciate what you have achieved.
2. Look at monthly goals and, when necessary, set weekly Gold Time goals that move you toward accomplishing each goal.
3. Consider each of your roles, asking yourself the following questions:
   - What's the most important thing I want to accomplish in this role this week?
   - What can I do that will make the most difference in this role?
4. Set one weekly Gold Time goal for each role based on your answers.

When I was talking with one client about this system, he had the following reaction: "It's not fair to have just one goal for my role as CEO when I have so much more to do in that role than I do in so many of my other roles. Why waste one goal on my role as father when I've got eighteen things to do as CEO? Can't I have more than one goal in this role and leave out the others if there's not as much to do about them right now?"

You may be able to appreciate this kind of problem. But it's based on task thinking and driven by how much there is to do. It is time-based rather than rooted in roles and personal values. The Gold Time system has nothing to do with time. It's designed to make sure that once a week you stop to consider your life and the roles you play in it. It forces you to place yourself in each role for a moment and select one important action to take in each.

Some of your role goals for the week may take only a few minutes, for example, "Call my mother." Others, such as "Write the first draft of chapter 3," might take hours. But time is not what the weekly Gold Time system is about. It's about balance in your life—living your life in a way that your personal values are not sacrificed in the pursuit of urgent, short-term "must do's." I came to see that my entire life could be consumed in this pursuit and I'd never get to what I really wanted to do. Writing this book is a Gold Time triumph for me. Your answering the ten Best Year Yet questions is a Gold Time triumph for you.

⬢ Having set your goals, put them in a place where you won't forget them and will be able to manage yourself to do them.

My experience is that the principal enemy is our own avoidance of Gold Time activities. Most often we'd rather pick up the phone or make another cup of coffee than do what's necessary to achieve the Gold Time goal. The only solution I've ever discovered is summarized by the D word. *Discipline* is what's necessary—the discipline to stick with it, past the need for a cup of coffee, a phone call, a deserved break. Avoid the call of the invisible hand that wants to pull you away from the most important work you want to do; push through the distractions of the mind until the thing is finished. This never seems to get any easier for me, but it works every time! Having put so much thought into developing a clear focus for the week, a little discipline goes a long way.

Makes sense, right? Again, perhaps the best thing to remember about doing what you know to do is to set up a support system to make sure you do it. When you meet with a coach, friend, colleague, or family member once a month to review your goals, you'll find not only that you are more successful in your monthly goals, but that you'll be plugging into the kind of energy and awareness that helps you to have your best year yet.

PART THREE

# The Best Year Yet Workshop

# Getting Started

Before you begin your Best Year Yet workshop, here are a few hints to help you get started on the process and make sure you are as successful as possible.

**1. Decide whether to do Best Year Yet on your own.** You may feel that you want to do this important work on your own, and this certainly works well.

However, many friends find that arranging a time to do Best Year Yet with at least one other person makes a difference. They know when they're going to do it—there's a date scheduled—and they feel less likely to back out or procrastinate. It can be fun as well.

Also, when you do the process with a friend, you have a natural partner to meet at regular intervals throughout the year for progress checks and support.

**2. Get in the right frame of mind.** I think of this process as time out for myself. I've spent a year in the river of life and now it's time to crawl out onto the bank, have a rest, and see how I'm doing.

Tell yourself how much difference this could make to you. A positive mental attitude helps to unblock the hidden barriers to new ways of thinking and behaving.

To inspire myself to make the most of these hours, I do everything possible to make it a stimulating and enjoyable time.

**3. Prepare your workspace.** Create a special setting for yourself. Clear a desk or table, make sure the lighting is good. Do whatever you can to provide yourself with surroundings that are as comfortable and positive as possible. Put on the answering machine or take the phone off the hook. Once you get into the flow, you won't want to be interrupted.

Years ago a friend passed on the hint that Baroque music is an inspiration as well as an aid to creative thinking. It's true. Anytime I need a boost to get going on a project, I play some Bach or Vivaldi. The effect is magical. Soon after I start listening to this music my mind begins to clear and my ability to concentrate increases. I feel that I'm in the flow of what I'm doing and more deeply involved in the project. My natural enthusiasm and motivation increase and I reach that state where I don't want to stop and I don't want to be interrupted. I forget my current frustrations and problems and get into the present moment.

We've used this style of classical music in Best Year Yet workshops, in a room where music tastes are varied, and the effect has been positive. Bach cantatas, Vivaldi symphonies, Handel oratorios, or Mozart concertos all work; if you don't have a tape or CD of this music, borrow one, or at least try listening to one of the classical stations and noticing the effect this has on your ability to concentrate and think.

**4. Gather your materials.** In the following workshop section there are spaces for you to write your answers to the Best Year Yet questions, but any pad of paper will do. You could also take this process as an excuse to start a journal, using a notebook or a blank book purchased especially for this purpose. Find your favorite writing pen or pencil and your organizer or calendar to serve as a handy reminder of what actually happened over the past year of your life.

Recently I've carried out my annual Best Year Yet workshop on a computer. For those of you who have the equipment and word processing skills, this method provides its own kind of stimulation and offers the advantage of allowing you to print out a copy of your answers as well as the final version of your one-page Best Year Yet plan.

**5. Consider these hints and reminders.** While it's possible to do Best Year Yet by staring into space and contemplating the questions, it works better to write down your answers. This way, the process builds on itself and you're able to do a better job. Awareness and consciousness grow, thoughts and perceptions become clearer, and important connections are made as you think and contemplate in new ways.

As I write my answers I often find myself thinking, "Oh, yes. I hadn't thought about that before now." Having a written record also lets you revisit your notes, flipping pages and adding to them in an ongoing process of stimulation and realization. Sitting down and picking up the pen is the hardest part, but I promise you that after ten or twenty minutes you'll catch the wave and be on your way. Trust me.

Allow space for one question per page, or make this book your journal and write your answers in the spaces provided. If you're using your own paper, write the question at the top of the page. In any case, start by asking yourself the question and then listening to the responses of your heart and mind. Write down whatever comes to you. Avoid the trap of editing and judging. Let your answers flow freely. You can change or add to them later, but to get started just let yourself go.

With each question, you'll come to a point where you dry up—there's nothing more at the moment. It's time to move on. You may think of additional answers later, so leave room for them.

Whether you're alone or with others, Best Year Yet is a private and personal exercise and you may find that you want to keep it that way. However, at the end there will be four answers that will form your Best Year Yet plan, including your goals for the year; you may want to share these with others in order to tap into their support and encouragement.

**Use the process of answering these questions to reach within yourself and be as honest as you possibly can. Tell the truth to yourself, above all. No one else need ever see what you've written, but it's important that you do.**

# Purpose

The first item on the agenda for the workshop is clarifying the purpose and aims of the workshop. Year after year it's been communicated in the workshop in much the same way.

## PURPOSE OF THE WORKSHOP

To make the next year my best year yet.

## GOALS OF THE WORKSHOP

Acknowledge and appreciate what happened last year.
Define useful lessons.
Create a positive internal focus for producing results.
Identify my top ten goals for next year.
Complete my one-page Best Year Yet plan.

# The Best Year Yet Workshop

Remembering the hints at the beginning of this chapter, think back over the past year and write your responses to Questions One and Two.

## 1. What did I accomplish?

_____

_____

_____

_____

_____

_____

_____

_____

_____

_____

# 2. What were my biggest disappointments?

_____

_____

_____

_____

_____

_____

_____

_____

_____

_____

_____

_____

_____

_____

_____

## 3. What did I learn?

As you reflect back over the past year, think about what you've learned. These can be life lessons you've become aware of and put into practice or lessons you could learn, given what happened. Just ask yourself the question and write your answers as they occur to you. Don't let a thought go by—put it down.

In order to remember all your lessons and potential lessons, look back at your list of accomplishments and disappointments. As you write your responses, state them as clear, straight advice— as instructions. Leave no doubt about what to do if you follow these lessons. Keep going until you feel you've mined all the gold available from your experience of the past year.

_____

_____

_____

_____

_____

_____

_____

_____

_____

_____

_____

_____

_____

_____

_____

_____

_____

_____

_____

_____

_____

_____

_____

_____

_____

_____

_____

_____

_____

_____

_____

_____

Which three lessons above would make the most difference to you if you followed them in the next year of your life? Select your top three lessons and write them below as your personal guidelines for your next year. Start each with a verb and make them as short and memorable as possible. For suggestions and inspiration, turn to the examples on pages 71 and 72.

**GUIDELINES FOR NEXT YEAR**

1. _____

2. _____

3. _____

4. _____

5. _____

6. _____

7. _____

8. _____

9. _____

10. _____

11. _____

12. _____

13. _____

# 4. How do I limit myself and how can I stop?

In order to have your best year yet, make sure the way you're thinking about yourself and your goals empowers you to succeed. A transformation occurs when you place yourself at the center of your life, creating your world rather than letting circumstances dictate your success. You can use your intelligence and your power to create a new reality for yourself.

The most powerful tool for personal transformation is the paradigm shift. A paradigm is a way of seeing and thinking about yourself, someone else, an aspect of your life—anything. Some of our paradigms do empower us, for example, "I've always been good at numbers." However, some are limiting paradigms, such as "I'm not the kind of person to make much money."

The next three questions are designed to help you discover how you're limiting yourself by having assumptions about yourself that lead to failure rather than success. Start by answering the questions below:

How do I limit myself?

_____

_____

_____

_____

_____

_____

_____

_____

_____

_____

_____

_____

_____

_____

_____

In which areas of my life am I not achieving what I want?

_____

_____

_____

_____

_____

_____

_____

_____

_____

_____

_____

_____

_____

_____

_____

What do I say about myself to explain these failures?

_____

_____

_____

_____

_____

_____

_____

_____

_____

_____

_____

_____

_____

_____

_____

Your answers to this last question are your limiting paradigms. With these perceptions and points of view, what results do you achieve? Where do they lead you? We feed these notions with our intelligence and awareness and then get results that are consistent with their inherent limitations. Life is a self-fulfilling prophecy.

Look at your list of limiting paradigms and mark the one that has the strongest negative influence on you at this point in your life. Which one do you really buy into? Select this one to shift to a new empowering paradigm for your best year yet.

Write a new paradigm that knocks this limiting perception on the head. Make sure that it meets the following criteria for an empowering paradigm:

- Positive

- Personal

- Present tense

- Powerfully stated

- Pointing to an exciting new possibility

Here are several examples:

- I empower myself to have what I want.

- I have the talent I need to succeed.

- In this moment I'm creating a great new future for myself.

- I'm able to go beyond my limitations.

- I've never been so healthy and alive.

- Whatever I put my mind to, I achieve.

---

**NEW PARADIGM**

_____

_____

## 5. What are my personal values?

Think about what's most important to you in your life. What are the hidden drivers behind your more tangible goals? What values do you want to demonstrate in your life?

Our personal values provide the strongest motivation for change and for achieving the goals we most want to achieve. Personal values are stated in one or two simple words that represent the principles that are most central to your life and who you are. Examples are values such as integrity, honesty, compassion for others, keeping promises, taking care of yourself, loving, and so on. Turn to pages 111–112 for further ideas.

To remind yourself of this foundation as you start to plan your next year, list your personal values.

_____

_____

_____

_____

_____

_____

_____

_____

_____

_____

_____

# 6. What roles do I play?

Looking at your life from the perspective of the roles you play provides an invaluable way of integrating the various areas of your life while placing yourself and your personal values at the center. Your roles provide the framework for goal setting and planning for your next year; examining them is the best way to ensure that you create balance in your life.

Write a full list of all the roles you're currently playing, such as mother, wife, daughter, friend, manager, and homemaker. See the list on page 122 for other possibilities.

You can add any new role you'd like to take on in the next year of your life, such as sailor, writer, poet, actor, student. Do you have a new dream role for next year?

_____

_____

_____

_____

_____

_____

_____

_____

_____

_____

_____

_____

_____

_____

_____

_____

_____

_____

Consolidate your list of roles so that you have no more than eight. Fewer than eight is fine. Integrate several roles under one title, if necessary. The purpose of consolidating is to ensure that you are able to give each role sufficient attention.

1. _____

2. _____

3. _____

4. _____

5. _____

6. _____

7. _____

8. _____

# 7. Which role is my major focus for next year?

Think about your personal values and how you want them to influence and direct the way you play each role. Look at the Whole Life Review below and use it to assess your *current* performance in each of your roles.

**WHOLE LIFE REVIEW: PERFORMANCE AND BALANCE CHECK**

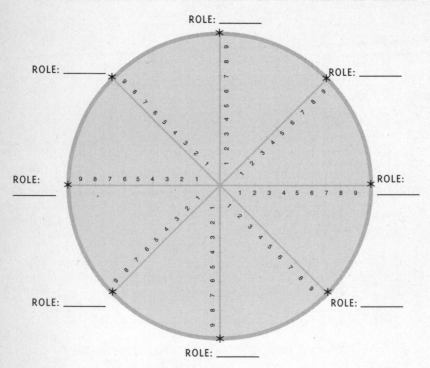

## How to Use the Whole Life Review

1. At the end of each spoke write the name of one of your life roles.

2. Notice that there are ten segments on each line. Use these to rate your performance on a scale of 1 to 10, with 10—the star at the end of the line—being the highest. For example, if you're completely satisfied with your performance, rate yourself a 10; if you're 50 percent satisfied, give yourself a 5. If you're not doing anything at all or your performance is abysmal, you'll probably give yourself a 1.

3. Place a dot on each line at the point of your rating.

4. Join the dots to assess your overall level of performance and to see a picture of your state of balance.

To choose your major focus for the next year of your life, look at the results on your Whole Life Review. Then ask yourself the following questions:

- If I could put one problem behind me, once and for all, what would it be?

- In which role do I want to have a breakthrough?

- If I were able to put a big check beside one of my roles at the end of this year, signifying that I felt a sense of mastery in that role, which would I want it to be?

- What's the biggest impediment to my success and happiness right now?

## MAJOR FOCUS

_____

# 8. What are my goals for each role?

Before you begin to think about a specific goal you have for the next year, take the time to decide which areas of your life are connected with each of your roles. For example, the role of homemaker could include cooking, decorating, paying bills, and so on.

Following are eight forms, one for each of your roles. Write the name of a role on each form. Fill in the associated areas of your life in the designated section for each.

Set goals for each of your roles, keeping in mind that powerful goals must:

- Be specific.

- Be measurable.

- Start with a verb.

You may want to review pages 146–151 for further information about setting powerful goals.

Once you've written your goals, check each goal to make sure that it is aligned with your personal values and that you're willing to do whatever it takes to achieve each one. If not, cross the goal off the list.

**ROLE:** _____

Areas included: _____ _____ _____

_____ _____ _____

GOALS:

_____

_____

_____

_____

_____

_____

_____


**ROLE:** _____

Areas included: _____ _____ _____

_____ _____ _____

GOALS:

_____

_____

_____

_____

_____

_____

_____

**ROLE:** _____

Areas included: _____  _____  _____

_____  _____  _____

GOALS:

_____
_____
_____
_____
_____
_____
_____

**ROLE:** _____

Areas included: _____  _____  _____

_____  _____  _____

GOALS:

_____
_____
_____
_____
_____
_____
_____

**ROLE:** _____

Areas included: _____ _____ _____

_____ _____ _____

GOALS:

_____

_____

_____

_____

_____

_____

_____


**ROLE:** _____

Areas included: _____ _____ _____

_____ _____ _____

GOALS:

_____

_____

_____

_____

_____

_____

_____

**ROLE:** _____

Areas included: _____  _____  _____

_____  _____  _____

GOALS:

_____

_____

_____

_____

_____

_____

_____


**ROLE:** _____

Areas included: _____  _____  _____

_____  _____  _____

GOALS:

_____

_____

_____

_____

_____

_____

_____

# 9. What are my top ten goals for next year?

Before you select your ten most important goals, review your responses to the first seven questions to remind yourself what really matters to you and why.

Review all the goals you've set for each of your roles and select the ten that mean the most to you and that will, when achieved, make the most difference to you. Once you have made your choices, check the list again to make sure you're happy with the balance of roles and values. Anything left out? Anything getting too much or too little attention?

Prioritize your list, putting your major focus first and the rest in descending order of priority.

---

**TOP TEN GOALS**

1. _____

2. _____

3. _____

4. _____

5. _____

6. _____

7. _____

8. _____

9. _____

10. _____

---

Rewrite the basics of your Best Year Yet plan in the spaces below.

## BEST YEAR YET PLAN

### GUIDELINES

1. _____
2. _____
3. _____

### NEW PARADIGM

_____
_____
_____

### MAJOR FOCUS

_____
_____

### TOP TEN GOALS

1. _____
2. _____
3. _____
4. _____
5. _____
6. _____
7. _____
8. _____
9. _____
10. _____

## 10. How can I make sure I achieve them?

You know what to do to achieve your goals. Write your first responses to this question. This is your best source of advice for making this your best year yet.

_____

_____

_____

_____

_____

_____

_____

_____

_____

_____

_____

_____

_____

The secret is to set up a system to ensure that you do what you know to do. Sanity and success are the result of doing the important things first.

Read about Question Ten, particularly pages 176–182, and learn to use the Gold Time system to win the game:

1. Set monthly goals to progress toward your top ten goals.

2. Set weekly goals to progress toward monthly goals.

3. Focus on roles and personal values rather than tasks.

Finally, empower yourself to win the game by surrounding yourself with positive friends and colleagues and supportive materials—anything that keeps you in touch with yourself and what matters most to you.

# Best Year Yet Plans

You might find it helpful to read several plans written by others to get a sense of how they have approached this most personal process. These men and women are from different circumstances and range in age from twenty-four to forty-nine:

**John, age thirty, financial planning consultant, newly married:**

### GUIDELINES
- If I want it bad enough, I will get it!
- If it is to be, it is up to me!
- Follow a daily regimented plan for success!

### NEW PARADIGM
*I do it to my best!*

### MAJOR FOCUS
Cheerleader

### TOP TEN GOALS
1. Always be positive.
2. Use W.A.M. (What About Me?).
3. See the "make me feel special" sign on everyone.
4. Begin and end all conversations positively.
5. Make love two times a week/foreplay one time.

6. Top the leaders bulletin each month.
7. Make Regional Vice President by 1 May '98.
8. Vacation with all parts of our family.
9. Do twenty minutes aerobic exercise and lift daily.
10. Check regimen daily before bed.

## Susie, age twenty-five, registered nurse, newly married, wife of John:

### GUIDELINES
• Make a bimonthly budget.
• Plan family vacations.
• Perform weekly evaluations of our business.

### NEW PARADIGM
*I'm more important than my list!*

### MAJOR FOCUS
Susie's coach

### TOP TEN GOALS
1. Give John a hug and a kiss every time one of us comes home.
2. Initiate the process of every Sunday morning performing our business assessment.
3. Make two or more trips home with John to see my parents.
4. Call Cindy once a month minimum.
5. Work out aerobically three times a week for at least thirty minutes.

6. Use Total Gym once a week for at least thirty minutes.
7. Relax and do nothing at least fifteen minutes a day.
8. Visit Darren and Leah in Iowa with John and stay three nights.
9. Call Darren once a month.
10. Get out of the Air Force by 1 July '98.

## Cooper, a bachelor and newspaper classified sales manager:

### GUIDELINES
- Keep my promises.
- Follow through.
- Pay myself first.

### NEW PARADIGM
*I love being an adventurer!*

### MAJOR FOCUS
Adventurer

### TOP TEN GOALS
1. Climb four 14,000-foot mountains.
2. Support Mom and Dad in skiing, camping, etc.
3. Get down to 215 pounds and maintain.
4. Camp ten times.
5. Quit smoking cigarettes.
6. Buy a new mountain bike and use it at least three times a week.

7. Support my girlfriend in healthy living and making the best use of her talents.
8. Write at least three letters a month and respond to any letters I get.
9. Initiate personal investment plan to save to buy land.
10. Plan and take three- to five-day rafting trip.

## Hannah, a fifty-three-year-old mother, grandmother, and acupuncturist:

### GUIDELINES
• Surrender.
• Trust.
• Keep opening my heart.

### NEW PARADIGM
*My magnificence is obvious.*

### MAJOR FOCUS
Acupuncturist

### TOP TEN GOALS
1. Establish myself as an herbalist and work in a clinic.
2. Create the financial condition to be ready to move.
3. Do one spiritual retreat.
4. Spend some time with my mother.
5. Attract a loving partner who fits and empowers me.
6. Be strong and healthy and keep my weight between 125 and 130 pounds.

7. Deepen my commitment to spiritual practice.
8. Have this year flow magically for me.
9. Increase my knowledge of herbs and Tibetan medicine.
10. Give up smoking once and for all.

# The Creators of the
# Best Year Yet

The Best Year Yet workshop would have been a one-off wonder were it not for the thousands of people who have participated in the process over the years and shared their thoughts, ideas, and experiences. They are the source of this book and the wealth now available. Here are a few of their stories. I've given them new names to protect their privacy.

Paul, a forty-three-year-old general manager with years of experience in large multinational organizations, is now in his fourth year of planning his life in this way. More than anything he appreciates the ongoing need to make room for Gold Time and says, "I'm much better at it, but it's hard." He says most of his success so far is a result of a newfound ability to tell people he's busy when he really has no appointment—only time set aside to do the most important activities. Paul says,

> I think there are about four phases in this process. First there's the novelty of the idea; then the guilt sets in, along with quite a bit of struggle to do what really matters. Finally the change really starts to happen and it feels like a rebirth. I'm looking forward to the final phase when it's all automatic—like brushing my teeth!

Hannah, a fifty-three-year-old mother, grandmother, and acupuncturist, is in her fifth year of this process. She appreciates tackling one main area of her life so it becomes the dominant theme in her life for the year. "Things happen over the year that are connected to this focus—many things happen, especially letting go of stuff I don't need," she observes.

She's learned to be far more flexible in the process and far less guilty when something doesn't turn out as she hoped. Because everything doesn't happen just the way she planned it doesn't mean there's anything wrong with her. Hannah says,

> *Seeing that I'm not living the way I want to be has been difficult. I have to admit that I've been postponing a lot of things that are dear to me. Now's the time.*

Joseph, one of the earliest participants in the workshop, who started by taking the course and soon was leading it himself, is a thirty-five-year-old CEO of a successful international consulting firm. As a participant in the process since 1981, he talks about having a much, much higher level of confidence that he can do what he needs to do.

> *The most important secret has been getting help when I needed it. I know that a large part of what holds me back is something I can do something about. But the most difficult part is not getting back into the old groove of limiting behavior—it's hard to keep this level of awareness over a long period of time.*

Another longtime player is Ann, a fifty-four-year-old successful actress and writer. Overall she feels her biggest win is that she's learned to make progress on the things that matter. For example, although meditation was an attractive notion for many years, it's now moved to being the focal point of her life.

*I'm getting more and more honest with myself about setting goals. When things are not working, I can now tackle it. But it's a gentle process of being more honest about my performance overall. After all this time I see that the quality of my life is far more important than success and achievement in one area of my life.*

Peter, a forty-three-year-old cofounder of a leading financial services marketing group, feels that sticking with this process for over twelve years has given him a strong competitive advantage. It's so important, he says, to get away from the process of day-to-day phone calls and "to do" lists and do the important things—otherwise they just drift away.

Most difficult for him is trying to do it on his own. Every time he's tried it this way, he's not done so well.

*The combination of peer pressure and peer support makes a difference—even though the people I get together with have no real bearing on the goals themselves. It doesn't matter.*

He too reports a shift from a life that's work-oriented to a focus on the quality of his life.

Finally, the experience of Michael, who describes himself as a fifty-three-year-old successful actor who's learning the hard way. This experience has helped him sort out a major difficulty dealing with the "stuff of life." For years he avoided really tackling both the problems in his life and his dreams, feeling a combination of unworthiness and disinterest. Now that he's learned to deal with this aspect of his life, there's more room for his inner self—the part that really matters to him.

*There's a new inner voice speaking to me. When good things happen, it says, "It's okay, you deserve this"—rather than the old inner voices, which warned me that it wouldn't last. The most difficult part now is that I get overconfident and lapse into a daze and then fall into a hole. Constant awareness is necessary and I'm not there yet.*

There are so many stories to tell of friends, clients, and family who have started to meet the promise of their potential. From day one my strongest motivation has been for people to see their gifts as clearly as they are seen by the rest of us—and to honor themselves by having their dreams come true. The world is a better place every time this happens.

Most people have all the talent, skill, awareness, and ambition they need, but it's often hidden under a cloud of self-doubt, past disappointments, or by simply being too busy. We rarely take time to examine what we're doing or why we're doing it.

The material in this book is designed for life planning through creating greater consciousness and awareness of the goals, targets, and objectives that are aligned with what you want for yourself in all aspects of your life. I hope you'll be happier, healthier, and truly more successful in all you do.

# FURTHER READING

❖ ❖ ❖

Breathnach, Sarah Ban. *Simple Abundance*. New York: Warner Books, 1995.

Buzan, Tony. *The Mind Map Book*. London: BBC, 1993.

Carnegie, Dale. *How to Stop Worrying and Start Living*. New York: Pocket Books, 1985.

Chopra, Deepak. *Ageless Body, Timeless Mind*. New York: Harmony Books, 1993.

Covey, Stephen R. *The Seven Habits of Highly Effective People*. New York: Simon & Schuster, 1989.

Dowling, Colette. *The Cinderella Complex*. New York: Summit Books, 1981.

Givens, Charles J. *Super Self*. New York: Simon & Schuster, 1993.

Handy, Charles. *The Hungry Spirit*. London: Hutchinson, 1997.

Hay, Louise. *You Can Heal Your Life*. Santa Monica, Calif.: Hay House, 1984.

Redfield, James. *The Celestine Prophecy*. New York: Warner Books, 1994.

Rinpoche, Sogyal. *The Tibetan Book of Living and Dying*. New York: HarperCollins, 1992.

Robbins, Anthony. *Unlimited Power*. New York: Ballantine Books, 1986.

# ABOUT THE AUTHOR

JINNY DITZLER has been a teacher wherever she's lived. She has taught high school, started two Montessori day care centers, managed and trained in the human potential movement, and used her personal experience in business to coach business executives in both the United States and in the U.K., where she lived for many years. Her corporate work focuses on consulting boards of directors to shift the culture in their organizations to one in which people are genuinely enthusiastic about contributing to the success of the business.

In 1980 she created the Best Year Yet workshop, which has reached thousands of people in both countries. She has personally seen many people through this process and trained many others to lead workshops and coaching sessions. The richness of these experiences inspired her to write this book. She and her husband, Tim, have two sons and now live in Aspen, Colorado.

## Want More Information About Best Year Yet?

After successfully starting a Best Year Yet workshop business in the U.K., Jinny has started a business in the United States to support people to have their best year yet, year after year.

One purpose of the business is to provide Best Year Yet workshops for up to fifty people at a time in an office setting. We have found that when managers and staff have made Best Year Yet plans that integrate their personal and work lives, they are more effective in getting the job done in their office as well as enjoying greater satisfaction in life.

For more information about scheduling a Best Year Yet workshop in your business, please call us at 1-877-972-7897.

Jinny's business also offers the opportunity for experienced trainers to acquire an agent license and to be trained to sell and lead Best Year Yet workshops. Licensed agents already offer workshops in several U.S. cities, but we're always looking for good people interested in leading workshops.

To see if a Best Year Yet workshop open to the public is scheduled in your area, or to purchase an interactive CD-ROM version of the workshop, please call us.